INVENTORY 98

12/13/76

JUNIOR COLLEGE DISTRICT
of St. Louis-St. Louis County
LIBRARY
7508 Forsyth Blvd.
St. Louis, Missouri 63105

D1161871

INVENTORY 1985

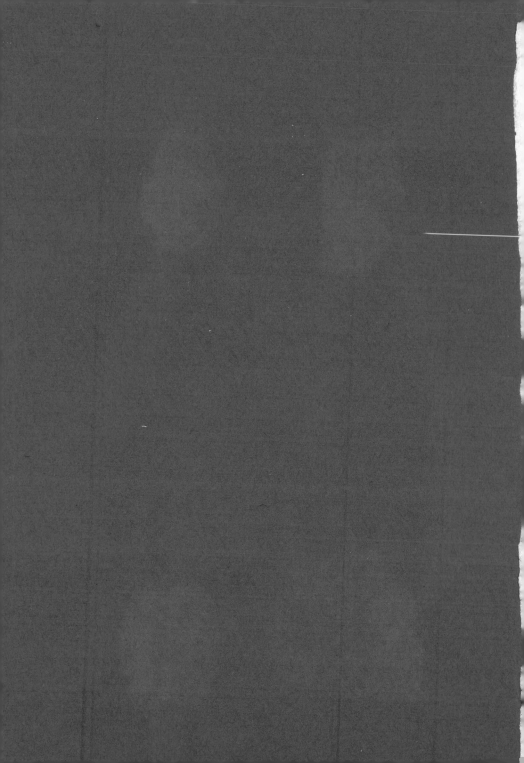

ERIC HOFFER: An American Odyssey

ERIC

Calvin Tomkins

Introduction by Eric Sevareid

Photographs by George Knight

Aphorisms by Eric Hoffer

HOFFER

AN AMERICAN ODYSSEY

E. P. Dutton & Co., Inc. ⊕ *New York*

1968

Contents

"It is a strange thing to be an American . . ."

—ARCHIBALD MACLEISH

Introduction

The first broadcast interview with Eric Hoffer on a national commercial network went on the air one Tuesday night in "prime time" in September of 1967. The next morning I was walking down the corridor of the CBS News building in New York City and a panting executive caught me up to beg me to arrange an annual TV talk with Hoffer.

Strange things had been happening during the night and early morning hours. The switchboard at virtually every CBS station carrying the broadcast had lit up like a Christmas tree. Now telegrams were arriving in job lots. Before the week was out the mass of letters had mounted higher than any mail response to CBS News for many years.

Eric Hoffer keeps no telephone in his one-room flat in San Francisco. I knew he would be over at the University in Berkeley on Thursday afternoon, so I called him then and proclaimed my fear that I had ruined his life; he was now a celebrity, God help him. He bellowed his laughter. "Ruin my life, at the age of sixty-five? *Nothing* could ruin my life!"

I think he enjoyed the whole business of the TV interview and the popular fame that followed. He has a huge body, great strength, and a gusto for most things in life. He enjoys nearly everything, except airplane rides. On an airplane he just blots himself out with strong drink until the nightmare is over.

This was not the first time Eric had been on television and neither television nor I introduced him to the American scene. His penetrating little books had done that long before. He was already exciting a lot of thoughtful people here, in Europe, and in a few other countries, India particularly, before CBS News got on to him. (I may as well confess that I had shied away from his books for years because Eisenhower had publicly praised one of them.)

For a number of months I had talked up Hoffer around the CBS shop, unaware that one of our producers, Jack Beck, was also trying to run the obstacle course of executives, air time, and budgets for the same purpose. Beck had flown out to see Hoffer, and to him belongs most of the credit; but eventually we got together and the various permissions were achieved.

So one evening in late May, 1967, we picked up Hoffer in front of his rooming house and took him to the bar at the Fairmont Hotel to talk it over. For some reason he and I quickly got into an argument about the psychological reasons for the lack of organized charity and the cooperative instinct among Latin Americans.

Suddenly I knew we understood each other and that he knew it, too; we were on the same wave length. Much later, after the interview had been filmed, he confessed that he had been very nervous about doing it at all because he really didn't know me, save from stray bits of my writing. But, he said, after that talk in the Fairmont bar he had called his "family" and told them everything would be all right.

The next morning we sat him down in a cleared-out hotel suite and ran two cameras on him for two and a half hours while he talked, sweated, gulped water, and talked.

I flew back to Washington absolutely certain that we had in those cans the greatest filmed monologue I had ever had anything to do with in all my years in television. But, knowing the corporate exigencies, I was disturbed. So I did something I had never done before. I wrote a note to my bosses in New York saying that if this program were reduced to a half hour and aired during the summer months when audiences are lighter and, supposedly, of lighter mind, I would do all manner of dreadful things to the corporation.

The program remained as an hour program and was put on the network in September, then run again two months later. The mail response the second time was just as big as the first time.

Hoffer had made millions of confused and troubled Americans feel very much better about their country. He had pulled aside the veils of supposed sophistication and, in new ways, showed them again the old truths about America and why they remain alive and valid. The purpose of philosophers, he says, is to show people what is right under their noses.

ERIC SEVAREID

The Creative Impulse

Eric Hoffer is a big man, six feet tall and massively built. Although he stands with a slight stoop, as if his large, nearly bald head were too heavy for his powerful neck, the years as a migrant worker and a longshoreman rest lightly on him. "Life broke most of the bones in my body," he says, "but it did not run over me." There is a brusque awkwardness about the way he moves, and a natural exuberance that keeps breaking forth in gusts, mocking his occasional claims to old age and poor health. His voice, which has never lost the German inflection of his immigrant parents, is resonant and strong; it shifts

1

dramatically with the ebb and flow of whatever he is saying, at times becoming almost inaudible, at times booming out with great force, the rush of words accompanied by vigorous gestures and trumpeting laughter. There is no doubt about his charismatic appeal. Hoffer probably could have become a mass-movement leader at any time during the troubled nineteen thirties, instead of which he became a student of mass psychology and wrote *The True Believer*.

The contrast between Hoffer the writer and Hoffer the public speaker is striking. On the lecture platform or on television, as the thousands who watched his first interview with Eric Sevareid can attest, his buoyant energy and warmth somehow manage to place all the emphasis of his words on what is good about America and American life. Even his critical remarks are delivered with such ardor that they seem to embrace rather than dissect the subject. On the printed page, though, many of the same ideas have a cutting edge. This is a question of style. Hoffer, who never attended any school, modeled his writing style after the masters of French classical prose —the principal model being Montaigne's *Essays*. "Montaigne gave me a taste for the good sentence," he has said. "I never had the urge to write until after I read Montaigne." The affinities to Montaigne are unmistakable in all Hoffer's writings—clarity, measured cadence, an occasional sententiousness—but the discursive tone is missing. Hoffer does not toy with ideas. His strong point is his capacity for bold and forthright generalization, an ability to go straight to the heart of whatever subject he is discussing, sentence by sentence, wasting no words. Every sentence is arrived at by a slow and deliberate process of shaping, testing, and refining over a considerable period of time, and the accumulation of these lucid sentences on the page makes for a prose whose effect is penetrating, weighty, and perfectly in keeping with the bleakness of some of Hoffer's ideas. Excellent instrument though it is, the prose may nevertheless come as a shock to some readers who, having discovered Hoffer

2

for the first time on television, go out afterward to buy his books.

Sometimes Hoffer is disturbed by the dark strain in his thinking. He likes to write aphorisms, short statements that sum up a whole train of thought, and he puts these down as they come to him, in a series of loose-leaf notebooks. From time to time he reads through the notebooks, looking for something to send to one of the magazine editors who constantly besiege him for material, and he is often amazed and frightened by what he finds. "It's fantastic, what terrible gloom is oozing out of there," he said once. "Because I'm not a gloomy man—far from it. On the waterfront I always used to think each day's work was going to go like a breeze. The other longshoremen there, they used to say that I had improved with the years. They said there was a time when I couldn't suffer fools gladly, but that after a while I got so I suffered them fine. Now I'm retired from the waterfront, where I wanted to work until the day I died. My stomach is not good, my kidneys are not good, but still I enjoy life, people, food—everything. And yet you put these damned things together and look what comes out: 'Most of us have done something in our lives to deserve punishment, perhaps even hanging. The knowledge of it, it is true, does not weigh heavily on our minds, but it is clear that no one has the right to happiness. We ought to get our share of happiness while we are babes in arms.' Or this one: 'A man's heart is a grave long before he is buried. Youth dies, and beauty, and desire, and hope. A grave is buried within a grave when a man is buried.' And yet, you know, I'm not a gloomy person. I've never been gloomy—not even during those eight years of blindness when I was a child."

Everything that Hoffer has written comes from a single train of thought, which was set in motion by the events of his life. "I'm not a professional philosopher," he insists. "I don't deal with the abstract. My train of thought grew out of my life just the way a leaf or a branch grows out of a tree."

Martha

Hoffer was born in 1902 in New York City. His parents were immigrants, an Alsatian couple who had come over from Europe a few years before and settled in the Bronx, where Hoffer's father made a meager living as a carpenter and cabinetmaker. Hoffer was their only child. His mother died when the boy was seven years old, and later that same year Hoffer suddenly and inexplicably went blind. As a result of his affliction, he never attended school or received any sort of formal education. At the age of fifteen, having recovered his sight as mysteriously as he had lost it, he experienced what he has for the first time on television, go out afterward to buy his books.

Sometimes Hoffer is disturbed by the dark strain in his thinking. He likes to write aphorisms, short statements that sum up a whole train of thought, and he puts these down as they come to him, in a series of loose-leaf notebooks. From time to time he reads through the notebooks, looking for something to send to one of the magazine editors who constantly besiege him for material, and he is often amazed and frightened by what he finds. "It's fantastic, what terrible gloom is oozing out of there," he said once. "Because I'm not a gloomy man—far from it. On the waterfront I always used to think each day's work was going to go like a breeze. The other longshoremen there, they used to say that I had improved with the years. They said there was a time when I couldn't suffer fools gladly, but that after a while I got so I suffered them fine. Now I'm retired from the waterfront, where I wanted to work until the day I died. My stomach is not good, my kidneys are not good, but still I enjoy life, people, food—everything. And yet you put these damned things together and look what comes out: 'Most of us have done something in our lives to deserve punishment, perhaps even hanging. The knowledge of it, it is true, does not weigh heavily on our minds, but it is clear that no one has the right to happiness. We ought to get our share of happiness while we are babes in arms.' Or this one: 'A man's heart is a grave long before he is buried. Youth dies, and beauty, and desire, and hope. A grave is buried within a grave when a man is buried.' And yet, you know, I'm not a gloomy person. I've never been gloomy—not even during those eight years of blindness when I was a child."

Everything that Hoffer has written comes from a single train of thought, which was set in motion by the events of his life. "I'm not a professional philosopher," he insists. "I don't deal with the abstract. My train of thought grew out of my life just the way a leaf or a branch grows out of a tree."

It has been a hard life but a remarkably full one. In its early stages, it brought him into contact with the outcasts of society—those he has described as "the weak and the poor and the oppressed, the disinherited, the fugitives and the undesirables in general." Out of this experience came *The True Believer*, a brilliant and strikingly original study of the nature and causes of mass movements. Hoffer identified the convert to a mass movement (the "true believer" of the title) as a permanent misfit, a person who felt for one reason or another that his life was irreparably spoiled and who therefore sought a new, collective self in blind allegiance to a holy cause. It hardly mattered whether this cause were political or religious, Communist or Fascist; the true believer was ripe for any effective movement that satisfied his craving for self-renunciation.

Now, seventeen years after it first appeared, Hoffer's first and most famous book has assumed an ominous relevance to contemporary events. It is not only in the Negro ghettos that the quality of American life today seems almost unbearable to many citizens; the general disaffection has spread through all levels of our society, to the point where a significant minority of American youth now look upon their national inheritance with shame and mistrust. There is speculation that the democratic system may be breaking down. Democratic government rests, after all, upon the willing cooperation of the governed, upon the spirit of consent and compromise, but today the polarization of American society between black and white, old and young, hawk and dove is so far advanced that the middle ground of compromise may eventually become untenable. The masses, the solid, stable, middle-class masses, see their daily lives upset and revolutionized by drastic changes of all kinds. How many may decide that a life drastically changed is a life irreparably spoiled? It is a time for true believers, and their numbers are increasing daily.

Although Hoffer is deeply troubled and dismayed by recent

4

trends in America and the world, he has only scorn for those who suggest that the country may be falling apart. His experience has provided him over the years with an unshakable admiration for the great majority of his countrymen. Hoffer believes that America is unique because it has been shaped by the masses in their own image. "America was not America until the masses took over," he has said. "Before that, you had a bunch of snobs running it." Because of the basic strength and intelligence of the American masses, whom he calls "the most skilled and competent population the world has ever known," Hoffer is convinced that the country will be able to surmount the current crisis of confidence and to deal with the terrible challenges of this period.

How he arrived at this conviction—how his experience was distilled into such a faith—is the subject of this book. Hoffer says that he will never write his autobiography. What follows, then, is a fragmentary record of a strange, strangely American life, drawn from a number of extended conversations during the last two years. "It's funny," Hoffer said recently, "I'm not even very American. I don't want the same things they do, I don't worship the same idols, and my experience has been so far removed from theirs. And yet, somehow, there is something deeply American in all my thinking." For Hoffer, this is a source of wonder and pride.

Martha

Hoffer was born in 1902 in New York City. His parents were immigrants, an Alsatian couple who had come over from Europe a few years before and settled in the Bronx, where Hoffer's father made a meager living as a carpenter and cabinetmaker. Hoffer was their only child. His mother died when the boy was seven years old, and later that same year Hoffer suddenly and inexplicably went blind. As a result of his affliction, he never attended school or received any sort of formal education. At the age of fifteen, having recovered his sight as mysteriously as he had lost it, he experienced what he has described as "a terrific hunger for the printed word"—a hunger that has never abated.

"What do I remember of that time?" Hoffer speaks of it with his eyes closed tightly, as though the effort of memory were physically painful. "Not much. I remember my mother was a small woman. I was a big boy, and she must have carried me in her arms until I was five, because when we fell off the flight of stairs in our house, I was in her arms. Two years later, my mother died, and I lost my eyesight. Did the fall cause those things? I don't know. I have an aphorism that says, 'We can remember minutely and precisely only those things that did not happen to us.' I've been asked these questions over and over, and it's all the vaguest, the most blurred thing in the world to me.

"What else do I remember? When I used to cry—and I didn't cry much—my parents would put me on a table and shove the table up against a cupboard with glass doors. And in the cupboard were books. My father was a small-town atheist—that means he was a small-town intellectual. He was a quiet person, very quiet, and he and I hardly ever talked, but he had all the paraphernalia, all the books that a German intellectual ought to have. Encyclopedias, dictionaries, books on medicine—the works. 'There is money in the cupboard,' he used to say—I remember that. And I would spend hours and hours playing with those books, classifying them, arranging them according to size, to color, and so on. I actually think my capacity for generalization manifested itself right there. And do you know that I taught myself to read both English and German at the age of five? My mother probably helped me—I can't remember. But I could read easily in both languages! I have a tremendously high opinion of the age of five, by the way. I actually think that to become really mature is to return to the age of five, to become able to recapture the capacity for absorption, for learning, the tremendous hunger to master skills that you have at five years.

7

I know that at the age of five if somebody had poured all mathematics and all physics into my ears, it would have stayed there. I always feel that I was a brilliant child at the age of five, and that I've been declining ever since.

"Anyway, when I was seven my mother died, I lost my sight, and Martha took care of me. Martha Bauer—she was a Bavarian peasant who came over on the boat with my parents. How she got acquainted with them I don't know, but the three of them came together somehow, and she lived with us. My mother died; Martha took care of me. She was a big woman, with a small head. And this woman, this Martha, must have really loved me, because those eight years of blindness are in my mind as a happy time. I remember a lot of talk and laughter. I must have talked a great deal, because Martha used to say again and again, 'You remember you said this, you remember you said that. . . .' She remembered everything I said, and all my life I've had the feeling that what I think and what I say are worth remembering. She gave me that. She was so *cheerful*. She used to stroke me, and comb my hair, and cook for me; all the food she cooked for me is still very vivid in my mind. When I was on the bum, and I used to get hungry, I could sometimes smell the meatballs that Martha made, out of pieces of meat, and egg, and bread crumbs. Not ground meat—she would chop the meat into pieces. And she used to sing as she chopped— '*Cim*barossa, *Cim*barossa. . . .' Something about when the soldiers enter town, the girls open all the windows wide, because '*Cim*barossa, *Cim*barossa. . . .' Oh, Martha must have had a good time. She must have been something of a hellion. How she came together with my parents I'll never know. I don't know how my sight came back, either—whether it was slow or fast. We were poor, and we had no money for doctors. I have the feeling that it must have been a blockage of some kind. And then puberty came, with the juices flowing—something like that. But, you know, I don't think I was happy when my sight came back. I was

8

being fed by Martha, I was loved by Martha, I was one with Martha, and then I got my sight back and there was—separation. And, in retrospect, it seems to me that I started to read then as though I wanted to ruin my eyes! I was reading ten, twelve hours a day—partly because I was sure I was going to go blind again any minute."

A secondhand-book store near his home had recently acquired a large library from an auctioned estate, and Hoffer proceeded during the next three years to read virtually every book it contained, becoming in the process something of an expert on botany, the previous owner's special interest, and on Scandinavian and Russian literature in translation. The very first time he came into the store, his eye was caught by the title of Dostoevski's *The Idiot*. It seemed to leap off the shelf at him, searing his mind with a memory of his father saying, soon after he went blind, "What can you do with an idiot child?" *The Idiot* was the first book he read there, and he has reread it dozens of times since, each time finding new depths of meaning. "I just read everything there was in that store," he recalls. "And to justify my presence there I used to buy a few books now and then. I can remember reading books by Selma Lagerlöf and Knut Hamsun and Jacob Wassermann—a German whom nobody reads anymore. Novels! I knew all about pâté de foie gras, all about the boudoir, all about champagne breakfasts from reading novels. I *love* to read novels. But, you know, when I read them now I feel guilty. Can you beat that? Because I can't tear myself away from them to take notes."

Hoffer knows that his father died in 1920, but the event is rather hazy in his mind. What he recalls far more vividly is that in 1919, very soon after the end of the First World War, Martha Bauer went back to Germany. "And how utterly callous can adolescence be?" he once said. "I always had the feeling that I could leave anybody, anytime, with no tug at the heart, nothing at all. I never wrote to her. I don't even know what happened to her. For the last twenty years

Martha has probably been more in my mind than anyone else, but in those days . . . Martha was gone, my father died the next year, and I was free, that was all. Martha had told me that I was going to die at forty. All my family were short-lived, she had said, and I believed her absolutely. Here I was almost twenty, my life was half over, so what was the point of getting excited about anything? I didn't have the idea that I had to get anywhere, that I had to make anything of myself. My father left a little money—about three hundred dollars— and I made up my mind to go to California because California was the place for the poor. So I bought a bus ticket to Los Angeles, and I landed on Skid Row, and I stayed there for the next ten years. You might say I went straight from the nursery to the gutter."

Hoffer took a cheap room within walking distance of the Los Angeles Central Library, and paid three months' rent in advance. He ate frugally, spent his days reading, and waited for a revelation of some kind. A strange excitement colored those first months on Skid Row. "There was the feeling that now every straw word would be filled with meaning. Hunger would have a meaning, loneliness would have a meaning, humiliation would have a meaning—no more straw words! Every word would be full of blood. Skid Row was just like a Jordan—you dive into it and you come to life."

When the last of the money his father had left was gone, Hoffer started to sell his books—the books he had bought from the second-hand-book store in the Bronx and carried across the country in a wicker basket—and when those were gone he sold his extra clothes. Finally, there was nothing left to sell, and he began to go hungry.

"I'd never earned a penny when I landed on Skid Row. What did I know about earning money? *There is money in the cupboard!* Then the money was gone, and so I started to go hungry. I thought hunger was something you were supposed to die of, but I found that you could go five days without eating. I watched myself— I've always been a very self-aware person—and it seemed to me that the hair on my body was growing faster than usual. I didn't *feel* worried, but when I caught sight of my face in a store window, I was surprised to see that it looked worried. And about the third day, when I bent down to drink water from a fountain, it felt as though there was a swarm of bees on my head. At night I used to dream about Martha's chopped meatballs. I was just waiting for the end to come. And then, on the fifth day, something happened. I stopped in front of a store where there were pigeons in the window— white pigeons and chocolate-colored pigeons—and it was as though the two kinds were segregated there. Just as I arrived, a small white pigeon was pushing its beak into the beak of a larger one, and I said to myself, 'Oh, it's going to be a feeding.' And then I suddenly realized that there was tremendous tension in the air, and before I realized what was happening I watched the ritual of birds mating. It's very exciting. On the waterfront, you can see it all the time. Anyway, I stood there at the window watching for maybe fifteen minutes, and during that time I forgot all about being hungry. So hunger wasn't so terrible, it wasn't so mysterious after all! It was no worse than a toothache! I felt as though a great weight had been lifted from my shoulders. There was a restaurant near by, and I walked into that restaurant just as free as you please, and asked if I could have a meal by washing dishes, and I got the meal. And out in the kitchen I met another man, another dishwasher, and I asked him how you got a job, and he told me to go down to the state free employment agency—he even gave me the address—and the next morning I went down there and got a job loading pipe."

The inertia that had paralyzed Hoffer never returned. He now found that his mind was exceptionally alert, and full of practical solutions. "I remember down at the state employment agency—it was kind of a depression then, and there were many unemployed—there was a big hall and a row of benches, with maybe five hundred men sitting on them, and another man, the dispatcher, in a little cubicle up front. The telephone would ring, the dispatcher would come out and say, 'A man to move furniture,' or 'A man to rake leaves,' and all the hands would go up and somebody would get picked for the job. Now, I asked myself, how come he picked this man and not some other? If I could only figure this out, I could have all the jobs I wanted. So I put my mind to work on it, and it seemed to me that the problem was to find the right place, to be sitting in the right seat so he would always see me. I tried the middle of the first bench—no good. Second bench—no good. I tried the sixth bench and right away he landed on me and I got a job. Okay, fine. Now, I always carried a book with me, and I used to experiment with different colors—red, green, yellow. Red worked every time. And I found that you should have an expression on your face as though you didn't have a care in the world. It worked like magic! Time after time that man, that dispatcher would call out, 'You in the middle,' or 'You with the red book,' or 'You with the big smile.' And so I got jobs. Not too many of them—just enough to keep from going hungry. And I lived that way for nearly ten years, reading and thinking and making a living on Skid Row."

Once, for a two-day period, Hoffer had the harrowing experience of being a businessman. He took a job peddling oranges and grapefruit from door to door in the Los Angeles suburbs, and discovered to his amazement that no housewife could resist his powers of salesmanship. The first sale nearly defeated him; he was so embarrassed that he could not say a word, and so grateful to the woman for buying from him that he cleaned out her vegetable bins before leaving. From then on, though, he found that the mystery of salesmanship was an open book to him. He sold out his stocks of oranges and grapefruit so rapidly that the farmer who had hired him was hard put to keep him supplied. At the end of the second day, to the farmer's disgust, Hoffer quit. "I could see that it was almost like a drug, and if I kept on taking it, I'd be hooked. It really frightened me. Because I realized that in order to clinch a sale I would do any-

12

thing. I could see myself telling those suburban housewives that I was a farmer, raised my own oranges, just cut them from the tree— I would tell any lie! And those poor housewives, how could they resist? So I told that farmer good-bye, no more. Maybe other people wouldn't be corrupted, but I thought I would be. Maybe I'm the most corruptible man in the world, and this is why I have always avoided temptation. Understand, I don't despise the businessman. I probably know more about the tremendous role played by the trader in history than you'll find in most libraries—why, the whole art of persuasion was invented by traders! I've written that the creative person is at his best in a society run by literate businessmen, by businessmen who appreciate culture, like the Medicis. But I just knew after that experience that I was never going to be a businessman."

The fear of being trapped by life, by situations beyond his control, has always haunted Hoffer. Toward the end of the nineteen twenties, he found himself trapped by a man's kindness toward him. Hoffer had taken a job in a pipeyard, planning to work there for a few days if it suited him. When he arrived for work the first morning, the owner of the pipeyard, a man whose name he recalls as Farbstein, looked him over with visible concern. Farbstein thought Hoffer looked pale, and he asked whether he was feeling all right. Did he drink enough milk? Get enough sleep? From that moment, Hoffer says, "I thought he owned me. I could no more leave him than fly." He stayed on at Farbstein's pipeyard for nearly two years, wondering how he was ever going to break away. Farbstein's death in 1929 set him free.

Hoffer collected the money he had earned—he had saved quite a bit by this time—and decided to live as he pleased until it ran out. And somehow, naturally and undramatically, the idea of suicide took shape in his mind. He was twenty-eight years old at this point. He knew he was going to die at forty—Martha had said so. What difference would a few more years make?

If there were other factors weighing on him at that time, Hoffer does not wish to speak of them. He maintains that then and for many years afterward he simply assumed that everyone, at one time or another, tried to take his own life. Having determined on poison as the method, he read up conscientiously on poisons in the *Encyclopædia Britannica,* then went out and bought himself a bottle of oxalic acid and placed it on a shelf in his rented room.

"I didn't have a care in the world for the next few weeks," Hoffer remembers. "Later on I wrote an aphorism that says death is no threat until it comes *tomorrow.* Anyhow, through the whole time I was living with a light heart. I read, I ate and drank, I got up when I felt like it. I was reading the Old Testament for the first time. And then, one day, the money ran out. That night was very bad, knowing that death really was going to be tomorrow. So, next morning, I put the bottle of oxalic acid under my arm and took a streetcar way out to the end of the line on Figueroa Street, out to where the big oil-storage tanks were. I got off. I walked a little way, and then I started to drink from the bottle. But the first taste was awful! Like pins and needles in my mouth. I spat it out and threw away the bottle and ran away from there. I had to walk all the way back to town because I didn't even have money left for the streetcar. And you know, in my mind still are the most vivid recollections of that walk back. Everything is as clear in my mind today as when I saw it. I remember passing a house and seeing a man and a boy on the doorstep; the son was pulling up his father's necktie and dusting his coat—details I'll never forget as long as I live."

The incident marked the end of Hoffer's life on Skid Row. Feeling that he had reached a turning point, he packed his few belongings in a knapsack and walked out of Los Angeles, heading south. Near Anaheim, a man in a flashy new car stopped to give him a lift. He asked Hoffer where he was going. Hoffer said he didn't

14

know, whereupon the driver began to lecture him severely on the need for goals and a purpose in life.

"He was a German," Hoffer recalls, "and like all Germans, he quoted Goethe. He said, '*Hoffnung verloren—alles verloren! Da wär' es besser nicht geboren,*' which means 'Hope lost, all is lost; it were better not to have been born.' And it bothered me at the time. I thought he must be misquoting, because it struck me that if Goethe was such a great man, he would never have said that. Can you imagine—I knew even then that hope is nothing to build on. I had learned on Skid Row that if you can't live without hope, you have no foundation under you. And so I stopped off in Anaheim and went to the library there to try to find out what Goethe really had said. They didn't have any of Goethe's books in that library, but they did have a book about Goethe by some Danish critic, and in there I found that what Goethe actually said was 'Mut *verloren—alles verloren!*'— '*Courage* lost, all is lost; it were better not to have been born.' What a difference, my God!"

The Fields

For the next ten years—the nineteen thirties—Hoffer made his living mainly as a migrant farm worker. He drifted over the whole state of California, sometimes following a single crop as it ripened, starting out in the Imperial Valley and moving slowly north with the other migrant workers, the Okies and Arkies of the Depression, until he reached the fields around Sacramento. Now and then, in the winter, he tried his hand at prospecting for gold in the mountain streams near Lake Tahoe, where three months' work with a hand sluice might produce three hundred dollars' worth of gold. He took

16

jobs with the forest service, and he became, among other things, an expert builder of stone walls. It was a grueling life but a varied one, and he was never tempted to leave it for the greater security and servitude of factory work. Years later, when Hoffer felt that he might be going soft on the waterfront, he used to take five dollars and a change of underwear, board a bus going to Fresno, and get off at any small town that caught his eye along the way. "The idea was, you have five dollars, you get a room there, and then you have to cut the mustard. I used to come back with a hundred and fifty bucks. I did it time and time again. Because, you see, I never had any sort of home really, and being on the road—it was like a home-coming. I always said that you could drop me anywhere in California, and within fifteen minutes I was going to have a job."

Skid Row had taught Hoffer that a man could live without hope. During his years of wandering, certain other ideas about man —man as an individual and man in the mass—took root in his mind and slowly matured. In his book *The Ordeal of Change,* he has described how the experience of living for a few weeks in a Federal camp for unemployed migrant workers near El Centro led him to develop his theory that it is the misfits who make history. There were two hundred men in the camp, and Hoffer soon realized that more than half of them were either mentally or physically crippled in some way. He had never before thought of himself as belonging to a distinct social group, but at this point he suddenly saw himself and the other men in the camp as a common species—the undesir-ables. "The majority of us were incapable of holding on to a steady job," Hoffer wrote. "We lacked self-discipline and the ability to endure monotonous, leaden hours. We were probably misfits from the very beginning. Our contact with a steady job was not unlike a collision. Some of us were maimed, some got frightened and ran away, and some took to drink. We inevitably drifted in the direction of least resistance—the open road." And yet, Hoffer mused, these

17

men did not seem below the average in intelligence; there was much tolerance and goodwill among them, and little viciousness. Given the opportunity, in fact, might they not be able to make something better of their lives?

The answer came to him a few weeks later, when he had left the camp and was crossing a stretch of barren desert on foot. It occurred to him that the pioneering job of making such a desert bloom would be just the sort of thing that would fire the imagination of every man in the Federal camp. "Tramps as pioneers? It seemed absurd," he wrote. And yet, as he mulled over the idea, it became clearer and clearer to him that the pioneers, those who left society and went into the wilderness, were probably people with the same characteristics as the men in the camp—men who could not hold steady jobs, drunkards, gamblers, fugitives, and outcasts, with a sprinkling of pure adventurers, young and old. "If in the end they shouldered enormous tasks, endured unspeakable hardships, and accomplished the impossible, it was because they had to. They became men of action on the run. . . . And once they tasted the joy of achievement, they craved for more."

It was clear to Hoffer, though, that if society's outcasts and misfits could become pioneers, they would equally well choose another path and seek a more sinister sort of regeneration. In Germany and Italy, for example, thousands of people were getting rid of their "undesirable" status just then by joining mass movements. The newly converted Nazi, Fascist, or Communist was more than willing to sacrifice individuality and freedom of choice if it meant he could also get rid of his blemished, undesirable self. Hoffer was later to point out in *The True Believer,* "When we lose our individual independence in the corporateness of a mass movement, we find a new freedom—freedom to hate, bully, lie, torture, murder, and betray without shame and remorse." The misfit, then, formed a volatile element in society, capable either of heroic individualism

18

or mass tyranny. It seemed to Hoffer in the thirties that history was being shaped largely by misfits who had dedicated their lives to the most dangerous tyrants of all time—Hitler, Mussolini, and Stalin.

There were, of course, many true believers among the migrant workers of the Depression. Hoffer remembers one episode in particular. "I had been up in the mountains for three months, placer mining, and I had just discovered Montaigne. I had the idea that maybe I might get snowbound in the mountains, you see, so before going up there I went into a secondhand-book store in San Francisco to buy myself a thick book. I didn't care what kind of book it was—it just had to be thick, with lots of pages and small print. I found just what I was looking for—a book with no cover on it but very thick, by an author I'd never even heard of. It was Montaigne's *Essays*, in the wonderful seventeenth-century translation by John Florio. And, of course, I did get snowbound, and I read the book through three times. How I loved Montaigne's language! I could taste the way he shaped each sentence, and for the first time in my life it occurred to me that maybe I could write something like that. When I came down from the mountains that time, I went to pick cotton in the San Joaquin Valley, and I was carrying my Montaigne around with me and quoting him all the time. It got so that when the workers wanted to know the answer to something they'd ask me, 'What does Montaigne say about it?' and I could look up in the book and find the answer. You see, what really impressed me about Montaigne—here was this sixteenth-century aristocrat, *Sieur* Michel de Montaigne, and I found out that he was talking about nothing but Eric Hoffer! That's how I learned about human brotherhood.

"Anyway, I noticed that there was one man in particular, a small Italian named Francesco, who was watching me all the time and listening to everything I said. Wherever I was, he wasn't very far from me. You know how we used to pick cotton? On our knees, with a big bag around our neck. When the bag was full, we'd take it to the weighing station and then come back. The bosses there had promised us good living quarters, showers—everything—but all we had was one faucet for the whole crew. No place to eat—we had to go to the store in town to buy food. And that first evening after work I was starved. I ran all the way to the store, I bought a loaf of bread, and I started to buy some cheese, and then here was this little Italian beside me pulling at my sleeve. 'No, no,' he said, 'You don't want to eat those things. It's not good for you! Come, you eat with me.' So he bought some hamburger, some spaghetti, some other things, and he built a fire back there by the irrigation ditch near where we worked, and he cooked up the best meal you could imagine. He even set up an orange crate to eat on, with a flour sack spread over it—a regular tablecloth! Next day, we started to pick cotton, and he was right beside me. At about two o'clock in the afternoon I said 'Francesco, you and I are partners. You go now and cook the meal. I'll keep on picking, and we'll divide what we earn.' And brother, for about two weeks after that I had the best food I ever ate. I'm still telling people how he cooked this and how he cooked that. So, then, what was his price? After I finished eating, I had to discourse. He had been listening to me quoting Montaigne, you see, and he must have had some idea in his mind about elegant living, something he'd seen in a magazine maybe—people sitting around after dinner and having conversation. After I finished eating, then, I had to discourse, talk interestingly, entertain him! It was not very hard, because I just talked about Montaigne, I talked about all I had read, and so on.

"One night, I was feeling particularly good—there was wine and everything—and I started to talk about the Italians. I talked about what a tremendous contribution the Italians have made to everything, and how all our civilization, all our music, all our culture we owe to the Italians. And then I said, 'Such a gifted nation,

20

and look at what that son of a bitch Mussolini has been doing to that nation!' The moment I mentioned Mussolini, the man froze. He just picked up everything he had and walked away. Mussolini was his hero. You don't know what Mussolini meant to the Italian migrant workers here during the nineteen thirties. Whether they were right to think so or not, they felt that the Americans despised them, looked down on them, and here Mussolini was twisting the lion's tail, he was throwing his weight around, everybody was afraid of him. And I insulted Mussolini! Francesco never talked to me after that."

To the other migrant workers Hoffer must have seemed rather a rare bird. Too solitary by nature to make close friendships, he spent his free time in the libraries—he had a card for nearly every small-town library in the state. And yet, he often felt the need to pour out in talk the ideas that were brimming inside him, to discuss with his fellow workers the books he was reading, to quote aloud from his beloved Montaigne and later from Pascal, whom he discovered in the library in Monterey. His exuberance led him to personify ideas, act them out, give himself over to them body and spirit.

Once, coming down from the mountains after an unsuccessful mining venture, he was stopped on the road by a farmer in a pickup truck. The man asked Hoffer if he wanted to work, and when Hoffer nodded, asked him whether he had ever sprayed pears. Hoffer said he never had. "Good," the farmer said. "I want somebody who's never sprayed pears, so you'll do exactly what I tell you." Hoffer was broke, so he tossed his bedroll into the back of the truck and climbed up beside the driver. He was to get forty-five cents an hour, and all he could eat.

The farmer was a Seventh-Day Adventist named Phil Hardwick. He raised pears, apples, corn, and string beans, and he lived in a corrugated-iron shack near a stream. "I still remember the first meal I ate with him," Hoffer recalls. "He didn't eat meat—I don't know why. His specialty was mealies, cakes made of ground

21

corn. He gave me a big plate of mealies with cream, and he had a big plate, and I got fascinated watching him eat. He'd take one spoonful of mealies and then right away he'd clean the bottom of the plate under it. When we were through, he said to me, 'Alec,"— for some reason he couldn't say Eric, he always called me Alec— "take a plate of mealies to the dog outside." Now, that dog, I don't think he'd seen another dog since the day he was born. Phil kept him tied up all the time, and the only other animals he ever saw were the horse and the rooster. He didn't even bark like a dog—his bark sounded like the rooster calling. Anyway, when I came out with the plate of mealies, he bared his yellow teeth at me, and I set the plate down in front of him, and believe it or not he ate exactly like his master! He took a mouthful and right away started to lick the bottom of the plate, although there was an acre of mealies ahead. I thought it was unnatural that a dog should be a Seventh-Day Adventist and not eat meat, and for a while afterward, whenever Phil went down to Sacramento to peddle his apples and beans, I tried to corrupt that son of a bitch. I gave him bacon, but he wouldn't touch it. I had to stew apples for that dog!

"Well, I worked for this farmer for about six weeks. Then one day we came back to the shack, and I happened to look at myself in the mirror. I looked wild. That's it, I decided. I went over to Phil and said, 'Pay me up, I'm quitting.' He gave me the money I'd earned, most of it in small bills and change. I threw my things together and ran. The bus was coming down from Lake Tahoe, and if I could get up to the road in time, I might catch it. And just as I got to the road I saw the bus! My hands were full of dollar bills, and I waved the bills and the bus stopped. It was like magic! I remember, I got on that bus and said to myself, 'Look, I've got a charm. All I have to do is give a little of the charm to somebody and they'll do my bidding.' The idea got hold of me somehow, and by the time I got down to Sacramento I was living in a fairy tale.

"What's the first thing you do when you've been prospecting and you get to a town? First, you buy new clothes. Brown tennis shoes, pants, shirt, new underwear. Then you go to the Japanese bath, and the Japanese barber and his wife get into your ears, get into your nose, they clean you all up. Then you throw away your old clothes, you put on the new clothes. Then you go and rent a room halfway between the library and the girls! I did all this, and I just kept on playing with the idea and living in a fairy tale. I had the charm! All I had to do was give a little bit of the charm, and they fed me, they did my will. And then, finally, after I had spent the last dime, all the charm gone, I went down to the San Joaquin delta to work up another grubstake."

The migrant workers accepted Hoffer's peculiarities without question. Only once in those ten years did he encounter serious hostility, and this was from a man he had never even spoken to, a Mexican migrant worker who came into the empty workers' barracks one Saturday evening, saw Hoffer, alone, reading a book on his bunk, and without provocation or warning pulled a knife and laid open Hoffer's thigh. Months later, the wound long healed, Hoffer climbed aboard a freight car and saw the same man cowering in the corner, dumb with fear. Hoffer ignored him. "I could have crushed him like an insect, but I had no desire for vengeance, none at all," Hoffer remembers. "It's funny, but I never felt I had any complaint against anybody."

Hoffer studied the men and women he met, and one of the things that impressed him deeply was the prevalence of simple kindness—which often seemed to go hand in hand with a sort of mindless cruelty. "I am always amazed by the kindness of people," Hoffer explains. "Kindness is not instinctive with me. I have a savage heart, ungentled by schoolmarms. I never learned how to meet people or behave with people, and I've always been such a soli-

23

tary person. With me, kindness is always an effort, something I have to make myself remember. But all my life I have found that people will go out of their way to be kind. Once, for example, I was going to pick hops near Healdsburg. You know how hops grow? Hops are climbers, they grow very high, and they come in clusters—very light, parchment-like things. It's easy work, and all sorts of people do the picking—women, children—and in the evening you get together and sing. It's very pleasant. I was going to this hopyard. I didn't know where it was. I just jumped off the train at Healdsburg and walked into town, with my bedroll over my shoulder. It was about ten o'clock in the morning. I saw a butcher shop, with the butcher in the window there; he was a tall, heavyset man with a white cap, scraping his block. I put my head in the door and said, 'How do I get to the hopyard?' He looked up. He said, 'Wait a second, I'll call them up and they'll come and pick you up in their truck.' So he goes over to the phone, and then he turns around and says, 'Look, why the hell do you want to go to work in a hopyard? You'll live like a dog. Why don't I get you a job right here, at Miller's dry yard right in town?' I said fine. So he calls up on the phone and gets me a job at the dry yard—where they dry prunes. I start to go out, and he calls me back. 'Wait a second, where you going to live? You can't sleep out in the hobo jungle and go to work tomorrow.' So he calls up a woman named Mary and gets me an apartment. I start to walk out again, and again he calls me back. 'How are you going to eat?' he says. 'They won't pay you right away, you know.' And he goes to the Greek restaurant right next door and buys me a meal ticket! Within fifteen minutes, then, I have a job, I have an apartment, I have a place to eat.

"I stayed in Healdsburg for almost two months. And then, one day, I picked up the local paper, and read about a trial just starting. It had to do with something that happened before I came—an ugly occurrence, when a bunch of vigilantes ganged up on some poor

24

Jewish tailor who was supposed to be a Communist. They riddled his house with bullets, and then they tarred and feathered him. And my butcher was the ringleader! He was on trial! The butcher who could do such acts of kindness was also capable of acts of fearful cruelty. You come to expect these things. . . .

"Let me tell you what happened to me in that dry yard. The first morning, I went to work near the dipping table. The way they do it is to dump two lugs of prunes in a lye solution, and then you spread them out on wooden trays, and two people stack the trays up, eighteen high. A lug of prunes weighs about fifty pounds dry and probably twice as much wet, so two lugs of wet prunes, on a tray, is quite a load. Anyway, myself and an Italian about half my size were working on those trays, stacking them up. It was fast work—the prunes come out, they're put on trays, you and your partner stack them up. I had a pea coat on, and when I started to get warm, I took it off. I got hotter and hotter. I took off my shirt. But the fellow opposite me, my partner, was just as cool as a cucumber. Not a bead of sweat on him. And then I saw something strange. All around me in that dry yard I saw people waving their hands, holding up two fingers, three fingers, shouting and gesticulating, and I said to myself, 'Brother, if you ever thought you had any intelligence, now is the time to get it to work!' So I watched my partner. And I noticed that while I was lifting the tray with both hands, he was putting his two thumbs underneath the tray and pushing it against me. I was doing all the work! The next tray, without his even noticing, I put my thumbs underneath. I pushed it against him, and the whole tray with the wet load of prunes went all over his beautiful clean shirt. I rushed over, helped clean him up. And from then on I started to cool off. I put my shirt back on, I even had to put on my pea coat.

"Now, what was going on there? They were betting! Betting on how long I would last. I found out that every morning the foreman went out to the hobo jungle and picked up a big man, and they started betting on how long it would be before they broke him —one hour, two hours, and so on. Well, I stayed with them, and they were the kindest people in the world. I never ate one dinner alone. I was passed on from one family to another, eating their homemade sausages, drinking their homemade wine. They even picked out a fairly good-looking widow that they wanted me to marry. And when the job in Miller's dry yard wound up, they lined up another job for me in the winery. I could have stayed there the rest of my life. And yet—look what would have happened if they had broken me. So it went; I saw it everywhere. These people are absolutely kind, but you've got to watch out. There is a kind of malice that is like a distant murmur in all of us—I've got a lot of aphorisms on that. This is probably what is meant by original sin, and the people who are involved with governing man should recognize that it is a fact of life, a fact of existence. But a *distant* murmur—that's important. Of course, at certain times and under certain conditions it becomes very loud, and then you get the mass movements."

Man, Hoffer decided, was nature's only unfinished animal. Eternally unsatisfied and incomplete, his soul continually stretched between the opposites of good and evil, he achieved nobility in the attempt to become fully human, or, as Hoffer put it, to finish God's work.

The Waterfront

All through the thirties, Hoffer was slowly teaching himself to write. He filled notebook after notebook with random thoughts and sentences, as well as passages copied from the books he read in the libraries. He even wrote two novels, one short and the other quite long, dealing imaginatively with his experiences on Skid Row and in the fields. During these years he never thought in terms of publication, though, and to this day only one other person has ever read the novels.

Toward the end of 1938, Hoffer happened to read an issue

of the magazine *Common Ground,* which was seeking at that time to interpet America to the foreign-born and vice versa. The magazine and its point of view excited him. Soon afterward, he put together his own notes and thoughts on the "undesirables" and sent them, in the form of a long letter, to the magazine's editor in New York, Louis Adamic. The reply came several weeks later, not from Adamic but from his associate editor, Margaret Anderson; she said that they were not able to publish Hoffer's letter, but that she had found it very beautiful, and had sent it to Eugene Saxon at Harper & Brothers. Saxon subsequently wrote to Hoffer, to suggest that he write his autobiography. Hoffer replied that he did not care for personal writing, and there, apparently, the matter rested. But that Christmas, Hoffer received a card from Margaret Anderson, wishing him well and urging him to continue writing. She sent him a card every Christmas after that—sometimes they would not catch up with him until months later—and her friendly concern, Hoffer feels, was what convinced him that he could become a writer.

"My writing is done in railroad yards while waiting for a freight, in the fields while waiting for a truck, and at noon after lunch," he explained in a 1941 letter to Miss Anderson. "Towns are too distracting. Now and then I take a day off to 'put myself in order.' I go through the notes, pick and discard. The residue is usually a few paragraphs. My mind must always have something to chew on. I think on man, America, and the world. It is not as pretentious as it sounds."

His usual method was simply to take a single idea and work it out in his mind, put down the result in fifty words or less, and then go on to something else. He can recall the exact place and the circumstances under which most of his ideas came to him. There was a period in 1939, for example, when he had gone down to pick beans in the San Joaquin delta, and was living in the migrant workers' barracks near Stockton. The barracks gave only rudimentary shelter. Hoffer's bunk was near the door, and all night a relentless wind blew peat dust through the cracks. His mind was exceptionally fertile and active, though, and when other workers moved out of the barracks and he could have had a better bunk, he did not take it. "I was afraid if I moved, I wouldn't be able to write," he remembers. Generalizing from this, he wrote in his notebook: "There is in us a tendency to locate the shaping forces of our existence outside ourselves"—a sentence that appears, unchanged, in *The True Believer*.

It would be another decade before this book took concrete shape. Meanwhile, Hoffer's life entered upon a new phase. The war in Europe had not only confirmed some of his forebodings about the mass movements; it had also helped to crystallize his emotional commitment to America. When the United States entered the war in 1941, Hoffer volunteered for the armed services. Turned down because of an old hernia condition, he decided as an alternative to look for "the hardest work there was," preferably connected to the war effort. He found what he was looking for on the San Francisco waterfront, where he joined the International Longshoremen's and Warehousemen's Union and started to work regularly in 1942. He was forty years old. Death had not claimed him, contrary to Martha Bauer's warning. For the first time in his life, he settled down to a steady job and a fixed way of life.

The waterfront, to Hoffer, was like being on the bum in one place. The men who worked there were infinitely familiar to him —most of them foreign-born, many crippled emotionally or physically; they were the same kind of people he had known all his life. His first day on the docks, a longshoreman asked him, "How's your brother?" Hoffer looked blank. The man repeated the question, and found it hard to believe that Hoffer was not related to Harry Almond, a gaffer (dock boss) who looked, the man said, exactly like Hoffer. Several other longshoremen made the same mistake, and so one morning, curious to see his double, Hoffer asked the dispatcher to send him to Harry Almond's gang. It was a disheartening experience. "He was awful-looking," Hoffer recalls. "Stout, wore glasses like me, had a big nose. I wasn't flattered at all. And you know, that Harry Almond was tougher on me than on anybody else."

From the beginning, though, Hoffer felt at home on the waterfront. There was a shortage of longshoremen, and the San Francisco docks were operating at full capacity day and night. Hoffer sought out the toughest jobs. He threw himself into work with reckless ardor, and his big frame absorbed punishment as a result. Broken fingers and toes, wrenched muscles, head injuries from working below decks—none of these slowed him up for more than a few days at a time. In 1943, however, a five-ton crate broke loose and fell, nearly killing several men and crushing Hoffer's right thumb so severely that it had to be amputated. Hoffer spent nine months in the hospital, getting a new thumb. The doctors took a piece of cartilage from one of his ribs, performed several skin grafts, and produced a misshapen but serviceable stump that afforded him full use of his hand. "I loved that time in the hospital," Hoffer says. "I could read all day. I was free. I was comfortable, and everybody was good to me." He spent most of the leftover insurance money that the union paid him on flowers and candy for the nurses, who adored him. He was delighted to find that it took the same amount of time to make a new thumb as to make a baby.

What Hoffer liked most about the waterfront was the freedom it gave him to develop and shape his thoughts. In spite of the pro-Communist orientation of the I.L.W.U. leadership, the West Coast docks have operated for many years in a far more efficient and democratic manner than their counterparts in New York and elsewhere. The dispatching system spreads the work equally and prevents anyone from monopolizing the best jobs. Frequent elections insure rotation of the union officers at the local level. The individual longshoreman is free to work as many days a week as he pleases, and

30

during the lulls in the work on the docks nobody tells him what to do with his time. At these moments Hoffer could usually be seen reading or writing in his pocket notebook. The other men soon took to calling him "Professor." He never once ran for office in the union, or sought out any but the most ordinary jobs.

It was while he was actually on the job that some of his best ideas came to him. He could be totally absorbed in the work he was doing, and yet, in the back of his mind, there would be a quiet place where ideas formed. Anything could start the process—a chance remark, a gull flying past, a partner's way of working. It was Hoffer's custom to work with a different partner each day, rather than with a "steady" or a four-man gang. He usually got down to the waterfront early in the morning so he could choose someone he liked to work with, but he was not particular. "I never ask that a man have more than one good thing about him," Hoffer used to say, and sometimes even a poor partner could start a train of thought.

Hoffer remembers with pleasure the day he drew the worst worker on the docks, a fellow so clumsy and inept that the others took pains to aviod working with him. "We went to work," Hoffer recalls, "and started to build our load. On the docks it's very simple —you build your side of the load and your partner builds his side, half and half. But that day I noticed something funny. My partner was always across the aisle, giving foreign aid to somebody else. He wasn't doing his share of the work on our load, but he was helping others with theirs. There was no reason to think that he disliked me. But I remember how that day I got started on a beautiful train of thought. I started to think why it was that this fellow, who couldn't do his own duty, was so eager to do things above and beyond his duty. And the way I explained it was that if you are clumsy in doing your duty, you will be ridiculous, but that you will never be ridiculous in helping others—nobody will laugh at you. That man was trying to drift into a situation where his clumsiness would not be conspicuous, would not be blamed. And once I started to think like that, I abandoned him entirely. My head was in orbit! I started to think about avant-garde, about pioneering in art, in literature. I thought that all people without real talent, without skill, whether as writers or artists and so on, will try to drift into a situation where their clumsiness will be natural and expected. What situation will that be? Of course—innovation. Everybody expects the new to be ill-shapen, to be clumsy. I said to myself, the innovators, with a few exceptions, are probably people without real talent, and that's why practically all avant-garde art is ugly. But these people, the innovators, have a necessary role to play because they keep things from ossifying, they keep the gates open, and then eventually a man with real talent will move in and make use of the techniques worked out by clumsy people. A man of talent can make use of any technique. Oh, I worked and worked on this train of thought; I was excited all day long, and I have a whole aphorism that came about as a result; when I got back to my room all I had to do was write it down. It often happened to me just that way—and all on the company's time!"

Hoffer's room was on McAllister Street, in a working-class district within walking distance of the San Francisco Central Library. Among his meager possessions now was a growing file of quotations culled from the writers he admired. His system was to copy each quotation from his notebook onto a three-by-five file card, which then went into a cardboard box arranged alphabetically by authors. Of the authors who accumulated large numbers of cards in Hoffer's file, virtually every one was French. "It's funny," Hoffer once reflected, "I can't read French, and yet it's the French who always influenced me. Montaigne, Pascal, Renan, Bergson—and de Tocqueville. What a pleasure to read de Tocqueville! They were my teachers. Among the English, Bacon. Dostoevski, of course, and Jakob Burckhardt, his book on *Faith and History*. I never got anything from Plato. Socrates was supposed to be a workingman, wasn't he? A stonemason or something. But this is not the way a self-taught mason would argue—he would tell stories to illustrate his points. How can you convince anybody by going after him the way Socrates did—another question, another question—showing him how stupid he is? I got nothing from Plato, and there isn't one thing I ever got from German books. The whole idea that anything that is profound has to be dark, has to be abstruse and difficult, that's a German superstition. They don't know what lucidity is. Well, maybe a few of them do—Nietzsche knew how to write, and Heine. But aside from those two, nothing. And the trouble with the French intellectuals today—Sartre and those others—they're writing like Germans!

"Of course, I think the biggest number of cards in there is on Renan. I found him after I got to the waterfront, and without Renan I probably wouldn't have written *The True Believer*. It was his *History of the People of Israel*, in five volumes, that got me going. Nobody reads it now. Renan has been belittled as a historian because he was too much of a psychologist, but when Hitler and Stalin came to power he was your most reliable guide to what was going to happen. He understood the religious mood, and his insights are really terrific. You can see in the *The True Believer* I quote him most."

Slowly and without conscious plan, *The True Believer* was taking shape. Hoffer did not acknowledge even to himself that he was writing a book, but increasingly, in the library and elsewhere, he looked for and found material that was relevant to his thinking about mass movements throughout history. His method of research was and still is somewhat unconventional. "I don't know the first thing about research," Hoffer once told a friend. "Listen, suppose you come to San Francisco looking for a person whose address you don't know. You can trace him by research. You look in the telephone directory, you go to City Hall; if he's a workman, you go to the unions; if he's a doctor, you go to the medical association, and so on. This is not my way! My way is to stand on the corner of Powell and

Market and wait for him to come by. And if you have all the time in the world and you are interested in the passing scene, this is as good a way as any; and if you don't meet him, you are going to meet someone else. That's how I do research. I go to the library, I pick up the things that interest me, I use whatever comes my way. And I believe that if you have a good theory, the things you need *will* come your way. You'll be lucky. You know what Pasteur said: 'Chance favors the prepared mind.' Take one of the chanciest things in the world, like war. Both Kitchener and Frederick the Great, when they were considering a general's qualifications, would always ask, 'Is he considered lucky?' It was a perfectly legitimate question, because if he was considered lucky, it meant he was prepared to take advantage of chance. I depend on chance to help me find what I need, and most of the time I've been lucky."

Although many of Hoffer's ideas came to him first while he worked on the docks, virtually all of them took their finished shape and definition in Golden Gate Park. Two or three days a week, when he did not feel like going to the docks, he would take a bus to the 10th Street entrance to the park and then follow his favorite path down to where the park met the ocean. It was a gentle, downhill slope all the way, with a minimum of distractions. The walk took him about an hour—just the right amount of time to think through the problem of the idea he always selected in advance—the "bone to chew on," as he put it—and when he reached the end of the park, he would sit on a bench facing the Pacific and write it out in his notebook, sentence by sentence.

A waterfront strike in 1946 gave Hoffer two months' leisure, during which he began the task of organizing his random notes on mass movements and copying them out in a separate notebook. The structure was a simple grouping, under four or five general chapter headings, of brief, highly condensed statements that were similar in length and completeness to the *Essays* of Montaigne. There were already a good many of these finished statements by 1946; even so, it

34

was two more years before Hoffer felt that he had something to show for his efforts. In the spring of 1948, he mailed the Introduction and the table of contents to Margaret Anderson in New York. "I didn't hear from her until the following February," he remembers. "I give myself a little credit for not being discouraged. Later I found out that she was in a very worked-up state just then. She had become the editor of *Common Ground* when Louis Adamic died, and the thing was falling apart just then. She told me later that her vitality was at its lowest ebb. Anyhow, she finally wrote to me saying she had sent the introduction to Elizabeth Lawrence, an editor at Harper & Brothers, and that Elizabeth Lawrence thought very highly of it. So I spent 1949 rewriting the manuscript. And when it was finished, I sent the manuscript and a check for one hundred dollars to Miss Anderson, asking that she type it. I didn't even know how to wrap up that manuscript; I had never sent a package to anyone in my life. I used to buy candy in a store near where I lived, so I went into the candy store and had the woman there wrap up my manuscript for me. Miss Anderson typed it, and sent it to Elizabeth Lawrence. It took them a long time before they made up their minds to take it."

When *The True Believer* came out in 1951, it was dedicated to Margaret Anderson, "without whose goading finger which reached me across a continent this book would not have been written." Hoffer did not take kindly to being edited. He fought stubbornly against any changes in the careful sentences over which he had sweated for so many years; at one point, he recalls, he sent Elizabeth Lawrence a scorching telegram in which he demanded that certain deletions and alterations be restored exactly the way they had been in the original manuscript. He got his way. On the other hand, the spirit in which he offered his work to the public was characteristically modest. As he wrote in the preface, quoting his beloved Montaigne, "All I say is by way of discourse, and nothing by way of advice. I should not speak so boldly if it were my due to be believed."

35

Lili

Critical reaction to *The True Believer* was astonished and highly favorable. Richard H. Rovere, *The New Yorker* critic, described it in a long review as a "work of almost pure cerebration and intuition," and compared Hoffer's aphoristic style to that of the Duc de la Rochefoucauld. Other reviewers praised the book's "icy wit" and "deadly parallels." Although sales were relatively modest, the almost unanimous enthusiasm of the literary establishment gave rise in Hoffer to a momentary euphoria. On an impulse, feeling that after so many years of living in cheap rooms and workers' barracks he could perhaps afford something better, he walked one morning to the fashionable Pacifica Heights residential section overlooking the Bay, and rang the doorbell of a large and imposing brick mansion, intending to ask the owner if he could rent a room there. A butler in uniform answered the door. Over his shoulder, Hoffer could see a parlormaid polishing a silver tea service. He asked to see the master of the house. "The master is in Europe," the butler announced coldly. Hoffer went back to McAllister Street, fully impervious thereafter to the corruptions of wealth and fame.

The book did not make him rich, and outwardly Hoffer's life remained unchanged. He kept his old room on McAllister Street. The neighborhood was changing rapidly at that time; large numbers of Negroes were moving into it, and most of the whites were moving out as a result, but Hoffer did not want to leave. He worked with Negroes on the waterfront and had no feelings of superiority. His requirements were minimal in any case—a bed, a worktable, a hard wooden chair. He had no expensive tastes in food, clothing, or pleasure, and no taste at all for property. As he wrote to Margaret Anderson in 1949, "It has always seemed to me essential not to own more than I can pack on my back."

The waterfront, in any case, gave him the opportunity to live as he liked. "It would be hard to find another occupation with so suitable a combination of freedom, exercise, leisure, and income," he wrote Margaret Anderson. "By working only Saturday and Sunday (eighteen hours at pay and a half) I earn 40-50 dollars a week. This to me is rolling in dough."

Hoffer enjoyed the company of the longshoremen he worked with. There was never any question of talking down to them; he admired their competence and common sense, and often used them as sounding boards for his own ideas. "When I was writing *The True Believer*," he recalls, "and I came to that section called 'Things Which Are Not'—the only poetic section of the book, where I say that from the beginning of time men have always desired the things which are not, the cities not yet built and gardens not yet planted—anyway, I was full of it. That day I worked with a Negro, and all day I was developing those ideas out loud. It turned out the Negro was a preacher, and the following Sunday he preached to his congregation on 'Things Which Are Not.' I felt good about that. You see, I always had the impression that there wasn't a single idea that I couldn't convey to these people. These men are so ingenious, so skilled, so highly intelligent—they can do anything. Look at the way they worked out that dispatching system all by themselves. Nobody helped them! They didn't need experts. I believe that the way to measure the vigor of a society is by its ability to get along without outstanding leaders; any organization that can get along without outstanding leaders is a good organization. Once, a few years ago, a professor at Berkeley told me I was wrong there; he said the vigor of a society should be judged by its ability to *produce* outstanding leaders. I told him, 'Fine, but it is precisely the society that can get along without them that produces them!' And we've proved that over and over in this country. After all, Eisenhower was the President for eight years and the country got along O.K.; it functioned, didn't it?"

Although Hoffer was well liked by his fellow longshoremen, he had made no really close friends in nearly a decade on the docks. Only rarely did he visit the home of another worker. Shortly before *The True Believer* was published, however, a longshoreman named Selden Osborne had sought Hoffer out and suggested that he come to dinner with his family. Osborne was an intellectual, a man unlike Hoffer in almost every conceivable way. He had taken a master's degree in political science at Stanford (where he roomed for a while with Clark Kerr, the future president of the University of California), and had gone directly from the university to the waterfront in order to exercise his political convictions—convictions that very

38

soon brought him into conflict with the I.L.W.U. president, Harry Bridges. Largely as a result of Bridges' enmity, Osborne had been thwarted in his ambitions to win election to union office and to rise in the labor movement. Hoffer did not have a very high opinion of the union intellectuals. He thought they were far from understanding the true nature of the working masses, and he suspected that what they really cared about was power. Nevertheless, when Osborne suggested that he come for dinner, Hoffer agreed. He telephoned their house a few days later, and spoke to Osborne's wife, Lili.

Lili Osborne remembers the conversation vividly. "The moment I heard his voice coming over so strong and with that accent," she said, "I just said to myself, 'A *paisano!*' When I was growing up—I was raised on a farm in the San Joaquin Valley, and both my parents were Italian-born—we always had an unattached bachelor in the family, someone who had come over from Italy to get work and who would probably go back to his home village one day and marry some girl and bring her back with him. So it seemed to me like the most natural thing in the world for the Osbornes to adopt Eric."

Not since Martha Bauer left to go back to Germany had Hoffer felt any enduring attachment to another human being. He had never come close to marrying, although this was not, one gathers, for lack of opportunity. His attitude toward women had tended toward the belief that they were of two kinds: those who were too noble and refined even to look at, and those who were for sale. Lili Osborne, a strikingly handsome woman then in her early thirties, warmhearted and humorous, a superb cook and a proud mother, seemed to bridge this gap for Hoffer. They liked each other immediately and without reservation, and it was soon the established custom for Hoffer to spend Sundays at the Osbornes' house. At the time he met them there were two Osborne children, a boy two years old and a girl of five; being with the children and watching them grow was a new and fascinating experience for one whose own childhood had been spent in darkness. When Lili Osborne became pregnant again, Hoffer made a prediction: "I say it's going to be a boy, his name is going to be Eric, and he will be my grandson. And that's just exactly the way it worked out." From then on, Hoffer's life would have a fixed center.

When *The True Believer* was published in 1951, Hoffer had assumed that he was through with the subject of mass movements. He had become interested meanwhile in the problems of the undeveloped countries which were seeking everywhere, with varying success, to modernize and industrialize themselves. "It seemed to me that all they had to do were a few simple, practical things," Hoffer said. "Build some roads, some factories, hospitals, schools. I wondered why it was that these practical things, which we do over here without even thinking, had to be carried out in the atmosphere of a madhouse." Hoffer spent more than ten years grappling with the ramifications of this question. A small volume of his selected aphorisms, *The Passionate State of Mind*, was brought out by Harper and Row in 1955,* but all through the nineteen fifties most of his efforts and energy went into the book of essays that would be called *The Ordeal of Change*, though for a time he despaired of being able to finish it.

Moving to a new room had led to a sort of creative paralysis in 1958. Hoffer had reluctantly decided to give up his room on McAllister Street, after seventeen years there, mainly because the noise made by his Negro neighbors allowed him only two or three hours' sleep each night. ("I had a whorehouse underneath and a madhouse above me," he said.) His old tendency to locate the shaping forces of his existence outside himself—the tendency that had once kept him from changing his bunk in the workers' barracks in Stockton—had

* Hoffer dedicated this book to Elizabeth Lawrence.

served to delay the move interminably. He connected his ability to write with the physical atmosphere of the room in which he had written *The True Believer.* "Every crack in the wall was significant to me," he said. "It was a real crisis." He resolved it finally by renting a room in the Chinese section of town, and one of the first things he learned was that Chinese children can be as noisy as any others.

Having come to a virtual stop on the new book in 1958, Hoffer began keeping a diary. He thought it might start his ideas moving. The entries in it are brief, and concerned mostly with life on the waterfront:

Eight hours on the dock. We discharge whiskey at a hectic pace. The sweating did me good, but my stomach is still upset. . . . During the day I kept thinking of Section 13. It should be possible to flesh it up and make it a substantial thing, with impact. I'm getting discouraged when I think of what is ahead of me to finish this book. Still, writing has always been adding crumb to crumb.

Got a book out of the library by Georges Bernanos. At last another genuine Frenchman!

What is it precisely that's floating about in one's mind during twenty-four hours? The days have a peculiar flavor because of some experience, of some spark of thought that flashed through the mind. Most of the time now when I catch myself I'm thinking of little Eric. . . .

At two and a half years, little Eric has an astounding range of understanding and feeling. . . . His attention is riveted on the outside world. He is not yet aware of himself as an independent entity, and keeps no book of enhancements and diminutions. He cannot be inflated, nor can he be humbled and crushed. He has a phenomenal memory for sights and sounds. He knows most of the letters of the alphabet, the names of a hundred animals, can easily identify any number of melodies, and knows quite a few nursery rhymes by heart. He learns rapidly, but forgets in a flash many things, even such as cause him pain enough to cry. He can be a pig and an angel in rapid succession.

In the end, Hoffer spent as much time on the new book as he had spent writing *The True Believer*. He considered many possible answers to the "madhouse" question. For a while he concentrated on the psychological effects of imitation; all undeveloped societies must imitate more advanced models if they are to modernize, he reasoned, and the very act of imitation breeds resentment. Hoffer had gone on from this to the realization that drastic change of any kind could *cause* a madhouse atmosphere. Broken habits, he wrote, are more upsetting than broken bones, and those who are thrown into situations of violent change are thereby turned into misfits. It was at this point that Hoffer suddenly realized he was still dealing with the old problem of the true believer: "I saw that change *causes* misfits, and misfits live and breathe in an atmosphere of passion, which is to say a madhouse." Somewhat later, it occurred to Hoffer that what he had been dealing with from the very beginning, in all his writings, was the problem of change.

Digging deeper, he came eventually to the conclusion that change does more than create misfits in a society: Change also brings about the need for a rebirth of some kind, and it is only those who succeed in being reborn who can survive intact the ordeal of change. He would pursue this idea further in his next book, *The Temper of Our Time* which came out in 1967. Hoffer considers this one of his most fruitful insights, although he is characteristically unwilling to claim that it is original with him.

The Ordeal of Change was published in 1963. In it, Hoffer's deep admiration for the American working masses emerged clearly for the first time in his writings. It was as though his long study of the undeveloped nations in Africa and Asia had released his unsentimental but profound respect for what his countrymen had achieved. "The deprecators of America usually point to its defects as being those of a business civilization," he wrote. "Actually, they are the defects of the mass: worship of success, the cult of the practical, the

42

identification of quality with quantity, the addiction to sheer action, the fascination with the trivial. We also know the virtues: a superb dynamism, and unprecedented diffusion of skills, a genius for organization and teamwork, a flexibility which makes possible an easy adjustment to the most drastic change, an ability to get things done with a minimum of tutelage and supervision, and unbounded capacity for fraternization." America, he argued, is the only real mass civilization the world has ever known—a society shaped and created by the masses in their own image.

The average American workingman was "lumpy with talent," in Hoffer's phrase. He saw the evidence of it every day. "Take those longshoremen—they don't think the fact that Hoffer writes books is anything to get excited about. Now, if I wrote a book, and the reviews said it was no good, I would get hell; they'd say, 'What's the matter, why can't you write a good book?' Of course, the longshoremen don't read what I write, but their wives do, and the wives tell them I write good books, so it's all right. But every longshoreman thinks he could write a book if he tried—and it's true, he probably could.

"Let me tell you about a friend of mine named Sanchez. He was just an ordinary longshoreman—drinking, gambling, talking, just like the others. And then one day he decided he wanted to run for vice-president of the union, and he ran and got elected. The intellectuals in our union—Osborne and the others—they nearly had a nervous breakdown. They weren't even sure that Sanchez could sign his name. 'How is he going to run a meeting?' they asked. Now, I've known Sanchezes all my life, so I told them, 'Look, if he can read, he'll get a book on parliamentary procedure and study it, and if he can't read, he'll get his wife to read it to him, and either way he'll become the union's leading authority on parliamentary procedure.' All right—Sanchez was elected. And, of course, it turned out that Sanchez can read, Sanchez can write, Sanchez can run meetings better than anybody else. Sanchez made a *wonderful* vice-president. When his term was up, he ran for business agent, and he made a wonderful business agent. Then, to confound all those intellectuals, he ran for publicity agent—that means he has to write all the bulletins. And he wrote the best bulletins that have ever been published on our waterfront. Not only could he write; it turned out that he could draw. He put out an illustrated bulletin! A regular Renaissance man! I tell you, the America I know is made up of about sixty per cent of the people, and I've never come across a book that says what I know about this sixty per cent. Every intellectual thinks that talent, that genius is a rare exception. It's not true. Talent and genius have been wasted on an enormous scale throughout our history; this is all I know for sure."

About the time that *The Ordeal of Change* was published, the effects of automation in the shipping industry were starting to be felt on the San Francisco waterfront. Most of the longshoremen there had little cause for concern about their jobs. Under an agreement negotiated in 1960 between the Pacific Maritime Association and the I.L.W.U., the employers had pledged themselves to contribute five million dollars a year to a fund designed specifically to offset the displacement of men by machines or by new work methods, and as a result of this remarkably advanced labor contract the West Coast docks, which had been the scene of so much labor unrest and violence in the past, entered the automation age with hardly a ripple of discontent. Among the sixty-five thousand members of the I.L.W.U., perhaps the only man who became seriously alarmed about the threat of automation was Hoffer.

Hoffer saw much more at stake than jobs and wages. For many years, he had been convinced that the common man needed work to prove to himself his own individual value, and he was deeply concerned for fear the coming of automation would deprive the American masses of the basis for their self-confidence and self-respect. Frustrated and uneasy, their talents and skills no longer needed, the masses, he feared, might become a dangerously volatile element in a totally new kind of American society—a society that would be shaped no longer by the masses but by the intellectuals. Hoffer was full of forebodings over this eventuality, for he was also convinced that the intellectual class had shown itself in every age as the worst enemy of the masses.

"I really thought that automation was coming terrifically fast then," he recalls. "It seemed to me that the most enormous and drastic changes were just around the corner, and that nobody knew what was in store, and that if these things happened and the people were not prepared, woe unto them—because the masses would be destroyed, and if the masses were destroyed, America would be destroyed. I really felt I had to save America before it was too late. It's funny, in all those years on the waterfront I never opened my mouth in a union meeting, never felt I had anything to teach those people, always admired the skill and ingenuity with which they solved their problems—much more ingeniously than I could have done. And then automation came along, and I got really frightened. I was *possessed* by the idea, and I started to run around as though the world depended on me to save it! I began talking to anybody who asked me."

Hoffer had spoken in public once or twice before this, in response to invitations from people who had admired his books, but he had been somewhat startled by his own ability to hold and move an audience, and for this reason he had given it up. Now he began accepting every invitation that came in. He lectured in churches, in schools, in Rotary Clubs and lodges of all kinds. "I would tell them that story out of classical mythology, that terrible story about the bull of Phalaris—how the Greek sculptor made a statue of a bull, a brazen bull, and he made it so perfect, so beautiful and lifelike, that the tyrant, Phalaris, decided he wanted to have it roar like a real

45

bull. And so, like God, the tyrant decided to use man as a stopgap for his own inventiveness. He had the throat of the bull constructed in such a way that if you placed a man in the belly of the bull, and lit a fire underneath, the shrieks of the dying man inside would come out sounding just like the roars of a real bull. And so they scooped thousands of poor slaves off the land and fed them into the belly of the bull—just as they have been doing in our own time, feeding men into the factories to make the machines work, using man as a stopgap for man's inventiveness. But now automation is coming to change all that, I told them. I said, 'Man is finally fighting his way back into the Garden of Eden! He was kicked out of there and told that by the sweat of his brow must he earn bread, and man shook his fist at the gods there and said, "I'll be back," and now, by God, he is coming back and spitting on the flaming swords that had barred his return!' And again, I had the feeling that I could move the masses, that I had those audiences in the palm of my hand. I could have done anything with them. I hated that feeling—I could see how Hitler was able to move the masses with his words—but I was possessed by this idea.

"I think, you know," Hoffer said, "that I have always had it in me to be a fanatic."

The fear of automation lasted for nearly a year. Then, little by little, Hoffer's faith in the adaptability of the American working masses reasserted itself. Automation was not coming as suddenly as it had once appeared, for one thing. Furthermore, like a good many other social thinkers, Hoffer came to the conclusion that all technologically advanced societies were rapidly reshaping themselves as schools for the masses, where all citizens would spend a large part of their lives in some form of education or re-education. The American masses, he realized, would probably manage the transition as competently as they had managed everything else.

Fame

Although he did not mention it to his fellow dock workers, Hoffer began in 1964 to spend one day a week at the University of California at Berkeley. Largely at the instigation of Selden Osborne and Norman Jacobson, a professor of political science at Berkeley and an old friend of Hoffer's, the university had appointed Hoffer a Senior Research Political Scientist in Jacobson's department. He was given a modest salary and an office on the top floor of Barrows Hall, where he could be found every Wednesday afternoon from two to five by any students interested in talking with him. From the beginning of

47

his appointment, although there were no formal course credits involved, students sought him out—up to twenty or twenty-five each week. Many of them disagreed totally with what he said. Some came once and never returned. But others found each session enormously stimulating, whether or not they agreed with him. Whenever Hoffer gave a lecture on the campus, which he did three or four times a year, the hall was filled. "He's charismatic, all right," Norman Jacobson said of him. "As one of my students told me after hearing Eric lecture, 'If he said, "Follow me," I'd go.' " Hoffer was quick to discourage disciples, though; his usual method, when a student too obviously sought his approval, was to tell him to go and write down his ideas clearly and explicitly, and preferably on one page.

The truth was that Hoffer felt rather out of sympathy with the attitude of the Berkeley students. He talked with a good many anti-administration rebels—this was during and shortly after the 1964 "free speech" riots on the campus—and to him they sounded like spoiled children. "Those so-called rebels," he called them. "I used to tell them they were fighting straw battles against a straw enemy, which is the university that shelters them. Let them wait until they get out into the real world and fight real enemies! But today they talk about growing up as something unclean. To grow up is to become corrupt. 'Don't trust anyone over thirty'—now, what the hell does that mean? To me, they haven't raised a blade of grass, they haven't laid a brick, they don't know a goddamned thing, and here they sit in judgment! Besides which, you know, they talk an awful lot of crap. I just don't see why we should go down on our knees and accept this nonsense and clap our hands. What is to be gained by humoring them? When they come to my office now and start to give me this line, I wipe the floor with them. One fellow thought he had written a masterpiece—*lots* of pages. I told him to put it all on one page and find out what it was he wanted to say and then come back and show me. He never came back. I tell all of them they won't be able to think clearly until they can write clearly. Some come back, some don't. It seems to me that this youth today is crabbed, bitter—but at the same time they know which side their bread is buttered on. They have an eye out for advantages, and they're not innocent. They all want shortcuts. Why take the long road? You remember Mario Savio, the one who led the riots in 1964? Before he learned what was what, he said, 'Why study history? We can make history!' And, of course, this feeling gives them a tremendous sense of superiority over the teachers who just have to teach them out of books. Today the only people who want to make history are the juveniles."

Inevitably, the experience of being with juveniles led to new insights relevant to Hoffer's continuing train of thought. It occurred to him at a certain point during this period that the juvenile mentality was strikingly similar in many ways to the mentality of the true believer. Juveniles seemed eager to throw away their identities in favor of a cause—any cause that caught their imagination even momentarily. They were prone to imitate, follow a leader, believe in magic, and they easily became members of a pack. The reason, assuredly, was that the juvenile was passing through one of the most difficult of all life's transitions, the change from child into adult. Most primitive societies recognized this difficulty, and surrounded the transition with elaborate rituals and rites of passage in which the young man underwent a sort of symbolic death and resurrection. The juvenile, then, could be seen as the archetypal man-in-transition, and, as such, he was a misfit; in order to survive intact he had, in a sense, to die and be reborn as an adult.

"And it struck me then," Hoffer said, "that the juvenile mentality is not confined to adolescence. There is the same situation at work whenever people have to adjust to really big changes—for example, when a predominantly agricultural society industrializes itself, or when people move from rural areas into cities, or migrate to another country, or even when they quit work and retire. Whenever

49

these things happen you get misfits, you get the juvenile mentality, you get a bunch of people living and breathing in an atmosphere of passion. Change turns people into juveniles! And until they can find some means of being reborn, as for example the early settlers from Europe were reborn when they came to this continent and started to build America . . . but I don't see this happening among my students. I'm just not very sympathetic to juveniles right now. Lili says that when little Eric gets to be a college student, I'll change my mind about juveniles. She's probably right."

Hoffer's friendship with the Osbornes remained the great joy of his life. He spent every Sunday in their house, on the edge of the Haight-Ashbury district that gave birth in the mid-nineteen sixties to the hippie subculture. From the time little Eric was three years old Hoffer took him for long walks in Golden Gate Park, and every Friday afternoon he met the boy and his mother and took them out to dinner and the movies—preferably a Western or a Japanese samurai film. Hoffer loves both kinds, and becomes so utterly absorbed in the action that he lives each scene fully, takes part in the battles, and occasionally makes such a commotion that young Eric, his sense of dignity offended, gets up and moves to another part of the theater. One evening, in a theater that specializes in samurai films and is therefore often visited by the three, Hoffer turned to Lili Osborne in the middle of the film and said indignantly that his seat felt hot. Lili looked down, saw smoke issuing from the cushion, and guessed that Hoffer must have accidentally ignited it with his cigar. She got him to change seats with her, and then went quietly to the back of the theater and asked the startled Japanese usherette for a pail of water. The pail was brought, Lili carried it down the aisle, poured its contents into the smoking hole in the cushion, returned the empty pail, came back again and sat for the remainder of the film in the wet chair. She had no choice, for Hoffer, once he had voiced his initial complaint, never once took his eyes off the screen.

50

Soon after young Eric was born, Hoffer arranged with the Osbornes to put his own savings into a fund for the boy's education. "He can go anywhere he wants," Hoffer says proudly. "Harvard, the Sorbonne—anywhere. And if he says the hell with college, he wants to be a longshoreman, that's fine, too. He has a good mind but a lazy mind. I used to worry about him all the time—I suppose when you really love someone, you worry. I was afraid that he wouldn't walk, that he wouldn't talk, that he wasn't growing fast enough. Now I worry that he doesn't want to work hard." There have been times when Hoffer's own intellectual differences with young Eric's father made things difficult for the boy. The arguments between the two men occasionally became heated, and this used to upset young Eric. Somehow, Hoffer feels, Eric managed to work this out in his own mind and come to terms with the situation. "He loves his father very much, he thinks of me as his grandfather. Right now he's not interested in me very much. I don't worry about him nearly as much as I used to." According to Lili Osborne, young Eric has become the only member of the family who "takes big Eric on"—who is not to some degree overawed by him.

Until two years ago, Hoffer liked to think of himself as an invisible man. He had, to be sure, published four books by this time. His work had been translated into a dozen languages; *The True Believer* had sold more than a half a million copies, and had become required reading in a great many college and university political-science courses; and Hoffer himself had become something of a public figure as a result of his lectures at Berkeley and elsewhere. In 1965, he had even consented to be interviewed for television by his friend James Day, in a series of half-hour programs produced by San Francisco station KQED and subsequently shown over outlets of the National Educational Television Network around the country. Letters from people who had seen and been impressed by these interviews came in from time to time, and Hoffer tried to answer all of them, writing on the same lined paper he used in his loose-leaf notebooks. The audience for educational television being what it is, though, he was seldom recognized on the street by strangers, and the outside world left him relatively in peace. He lived alone, as always, in a single bare room with no telephone and a bed that folded up in the closet. Until the spring of 1967 he still worked three days a week on the waterfront, where his literary career excited no special attention. He continued to spend his free time reading, writing, walking in the park, and seeing the Osbornes. Hoffer's relative invisibility ended forever on the evening of September 19, though, when his one-hour televised conversation with Eric Sevareid was shown nationally over the CBS network.

There is certainly no single explanation for the public response to this first Hoffer-Sevareid interview (the program was repeated on November 14, 1967). Sevareid, who says that the mail and the telephone calls to the network exceeded anything he had seen during his career in broadcasting, has ascribed the program's tremendous impact to Hoffer's having "touched the nerve of faith about ourselves and our nation." Others—Lili Osborne among them—attribute it partly, at least, to the emotional and physical appeal of the man himself: Here was an authentic face, something rarely seen on television, and here was an authentic man whose words sprang from deep and passionately felt experience. Lili Osborne's view is borne out by some of the mail that has continued in inundate Hoffer ever since the program. A great many of the letters are from women, and the ardor of their phrasing is unmistakable: "I wish I could embrace you," a Washington, D.C., housewife wrote, "for I would feel that I was embracing all of the very best that is in America." On the other hand, there have been a surprising number of letters from young people—servicemen in particular—some argumentative, but the majority full of respect and gratitude. It would seem, in any case, that Hoffer managed to touch a number of different nerves that evening, and that the response was by no means limited to what he said.

Hoffer soon gave up trying to answer all his mail. The vast majority of the letters he has received since the program contain invitations to lecture, to teach, to take part in seminars or conferences, and most of these he simply ignores. "They got along fine without me before," he notes, "and I don't have any special message to deliver to anyone." Occasionally, if a letter is especially persuasive, he will accept a speaking engagement. He rather enjoys going to small, backwoods community colleges, which he tends to look upon as the prototypes of the "schools for the masses" that will carry out the common man's future transition from manual to intellectual work. For a while he accepted engagements that were two years or more in the future, assuming that he would probably be dead by then anyway; now that he has had to make good on several of these long-term invitations, he has grown more cautious.

Among the groups and organizations that seek him out, Hoffer says, the most persistent are the Jesuits, the Jews, and the psychiatrists. "Every day I get letters from monsignors, from bishops—and I am a nonbeliever!" Hoffer shouts with delight at the irony. "They tell me I am a theologian. My theology is theology of the soul, you see—I believe that God and the devil are fighting their battle, not in heaven but in man's soul. And I have a definition of God—anything that humanizes is God, anything that dehumanizes is the devil. They love that! They pass the word around, so wherever the Jesuits are, I am a hero. And Lili's family down there in the San Joaquin Valley—they are all very pious Catholics; they always looked askance at me as an unbeliever, as a corrupting influence. But now, since all the monsignors and the bishops are after me, I'm a hero to Lili's family! I get letters from them addressed to 'Eric Cardinal Hoffer,' beginning 'Your Eminence!'

"Now, of course, if you want immortality, all you have to

do is say something for the Jews or against the Jews, and they'll never forget you. In my writing I give credit to the Jews for placing man in opposition to nature for the first time in history. It was the Jews who said you don't just submit to the laws of nature, you are supposed to browbeat them, to subdue them. And so they write to me.

"As for the psychiatrists—well, I never read a book on psychiatry in my life, not even Freud. What the hell could Freud teach me? Freud lived in a tight little community, Vienna, and within that was the Jewish community, even tighter, and within the Jewish community was the Freud family, tighter yet, and naturally there was a great deal of suppression and all that. In my case there was never any suppression. Nothing! The same with most of the people I work with. Once, a man sent me a pre-publication copy of his book, called *Everyday Neurosis*. I sent it right back with a note saying, 'Dear Sir, the people I live with have money trouble, not neurosis, and if they have a neurosis it's a neurosis that money will cure.' And yet, you see, it seems that I talk about the same things the psychiatrists talk about, but without the jargon. I have this idea about man fighting nature on two fronts. There is nature around you, which you have to combat in order to make a living; and there is nature within you, the animal lusts, the part that Freud talked about. So you are fighting nature on two fronts. But here is a terrible thing: When you win on one front, you lose on the other! The triumph of the engineer brings affluence, brings victory over external nature, but it also sets up the stage for the psychiatrist. On the other hand, if you win the war against nature inside you, and end up with a population of yogis and ascetics, you are going to starve in the street. The idea, of course, is not to win on either front. Man needs that tension, that stretching of the soul between two polarities—I have a pretty good aphorism on that, by the way. Anyhow, you ought to see the invitations I get now from the psychiatrists."

Of all the invitations that came as a result of the CBS broadcast, though, the one that has meant the most to Hoffer came from the White House. In the course of his interview with Sevareid, Hoffer had said that he thought Lyndon Johnson would go down in history as "the foremost President of the twentieth century." For a beleaguered Chief Executive who had derived very little comfort from the popularity polls in the preceding months, this was an unexpected and welcome boost. Johnson quoted Hoffer in a speech three days later, and within two weeks of the CBS interview, Hoffer and Johnson were photographed together, chatting cozily on the White House lawn.

"I was supposed to spend five minutes with him," Hoffer said later. "Just shake hands and so forth. We spent fifty minutes. I don't even remember what we talked about, except that once I said, 'Isn't it wonderful that a Johnson can become President?' The people around us, they seemed to think I had put my foot in it or something, but not Johnson. He said, 'You're darned right!' Oh, I treated him like a beautiful woman; I had eyes only for Johnson. And I'm not a young girl to be bowled over by these things, but that day, for the first time in my life, I had a sense of history."

To many people it seemed almost inconceivable that a mind noted for its critical bite and historical penetration should be so uncritically admiring of Lyndon Johnson. (It was to the man himself, not simply the office, that Hoffer responded. When Eisenhower, during his first term as President, became an admirer of *The True Believer* and began handing out copies of the book to friends and associates, Hoffer was not particularly flattered. "It proved to me something I always knew," he said once, "which is that this is the kind of book any child can read.")

In the case of Johnson, Hoffer's commitment appeared to be primarily emotional and instinctive. Hoffer felt immediately at home with Johnson. "It was just like seeing a longshoreman become President," he said. "Johnson is so familiar to me—I've worked with Johnsons all my life. Why, he could come down on the waterfront tomorrow, and in five minutes you wouldn't be able to tell him from anyone else."

55

The meeting confirmed Hoffer's vision of Johnson as the protagonist in the great spiritual drama of the American common man.

And yet, when Hoffer talks today about Vietnam and the other critical problems this country faces, he is full of doubts and forebodings. He is deeply worried about the decay and disruption of urban life, about the plague of drugs that he sees as the precipitate of the hippie movement, about the plight of the Negro in America. The Negro must undergo a sense of rebirth in order to assume his rightful place in society, Hoffer has said; he can do this by giving birth to communities and enterprises that are his own—black unions, rebuilt neighborhoods, local organizations created by and for Negroes, out of which he can draw a sense of pride in himself. "The Negro has to have the sense of being a new man," Hoffer says, "of being altogether different from what he was yesterday. But, of course, how can he do this as long as he is always a Negro first and only secondly an individual? If you knew that Jesus Christ was coming in the door, and it turned out that Jesus Christ was a Negro, you would see the Negro before you saw Jesus Christ. It's as bad as that."

As far as Vietnam is concerned, Hoffer has often said that the United States was not there to fight Communism, but to prevent a third world war. "I'm not afraid of Communism, in Asia or any-where else," he said recently. "I wouldn't stop the Communists from taking over all of South America if they tried. The real trouble in South America is the rich—you have a species of rich there who are not concerned about anybody but themselves, and who are draining those countries of their wealth, and we don't know how to get rid of them. Let the Communists take over down there, and then fight among themselves! On the waterfront, you know, the Communists all end up as successful real-estate dealers. No, I'm not afraid of Communism; what I'm afraid of is a third world war. Johnson was convinced that he was stopping a third world war by being in Vietnam. And he didn't get into Vietnam to begin with—three administrations have been convinced that you had to have a toehold in East Asia in order to stabilize the Pacific. But what do I know about what is going on in Vietnam today? Sometimes I pick up the paper and wonder whether we have one intelligent man among the Americans in Vietnam. And I am afraid of defeat there. Not because we are going to be humiliated, but because of what defeat is going to do to us. Those stupid intellectuals on the Berkeley campus are saying, 'After defeat, we come—there's going to be a social revolution.' But they're wrong. After defeat, there's going to be Hitler here. This is the pattern of defeat in this country. Look what happened in the South after the Civil War—after defeat, the Ku Klux Klan. Look what happened after partial defeat in Korea—you had McCarthy. Defeat in Vietnam—why, the legend of the stab in the back is already so well documented. They'll be able to quote what this fellow said, how that one burned his draft card, how they prevented shipping, how they prevented induction, how they went to Ho Chi Minh and said they were behind him. . . . Of course it's not going to be a German type, but if any Hitler rises in this country, he's going to have everything his own way."

Now and then, when the world outside seems to weigh most heavily on him, Hoffer dreams of going off by himself to a place where no one knows him, a cabin in the Ozarks, perhaps, where he could spend the last years of his life quietly and simply, "eating, drinking, reading novels, maybe even fishing—something I've never done, by the way. If it weren't for Lili and little Eric, this is probably what I would do," he said, one evening recently, after dinner at the Osbornes' house. "But I think even if I should go to the North Pole, Lili would come and find me and bring me back here."

"That's true," she agreed, laughing. "I probably would. We love Eric."

"Can you beat that?" Hoffer said, in what sounded like genuine amazement.

Americans

Hoffer had fully expected to go on working on the waterfront until the day he died. He had always believed that active, physical labor was a necessity for him, as a stimulus to his mind, and although he worked only three days a week as he grew older and did not really need the money he made on the docks, he had somehow hoped that he would be able to stay on the job after reaching retirement age. His first pension check, in April, 1967, came as a heavy blow. For more than a year afterward he could not bring himself to go back and visit his old friends on the docks. He was afraid, he said, that there might be resentment of the publicity surrounding his television appearance, but more than that he was afraid of stirring up his own memories. "I miss it very much," he admitted sadly. "These are the only people I know. And how many times I get up in the morning and I am so tired, because I've been loading and unloading the ships all night in my sleep."

His life in retirement has been more solitary than ever. Most mornings, he gets up early, has his breakfast at Blum's on the corner of Polk and California streets, then takes a long walk through the city, six miles or more in good weather. He is a "self-appointed inspector of buildings" in San Francisco, a close student of the ways in which the city is rebuilding and reshaping itself.

Not too long ago he was taken by a friend to meet one of the designers at the architectural firm of Skidmore, Owings & Merrill, whose new building at One Maritime Plaza Hoffer had particularly admired. Dressed as always in a pea jacket and clean work pants, he burst into the elegant, gleaming suite of offices like a March wind, ruffling the secretaries and practically shouting his enthusiasm for the building. When the designer, a little later in their conversation, began to talk about the function of the architect in relating structures to the total environment, Hoffer took immediate and exuberant issue with him. Architecture, he said, should stand out against the environment; nature was not to be related or conformed to, but overwhelmed and subdued. The argument boiled back and forth for nearly an hour before Hoffer took his leave.

After the morning walk, Hoffer usually goes back to his room and reads or writes for an hour or two. He is following a new train of thought—actually, a continuation of the old one—which has to do with the creative situation in human life.

"The creative periods in history—that's what interests me now," he explains. "What happened in Athens at the time of Pericles? What happened in Florence during the Renaissance? What happened in Rembrandt's Amsterdam and Shakespeare's London? These sudden outpourings of talent and genius on the part of people who seem no different from anyone else—how do you explain them? And what causes them to die out so quickly? All the things you hear about the need for faith, the need for national goals and ideals—it's all nonsense. You don't need faith. And the trivial things are so important, the toys that men set their hearts on. The trivial things are not trivial! And you know, I've found that everything creative comes from the city. All men's theories and great achievements— they were not realized in the bracing atmosphere of forests and steppes and mountaintops, but in the crowded, stinking cities! Nothing of importance has ever come from the village—how could anything be invented in places where strangers are not welcome? Man became human in the city; without the city, man would have been nothing. And, of course, it's in the cities that man decays, too. America will die if we don't know how to run viable cities."

In his mind's eye, Hoffer sees the development of neighborhoods as the answer to the problem of unlivable cities. Brute megalopolis must be articulated into individual units, each with its own shape and style and independence. To Hoffer, a neighborhood is a place of congregation, a place where people who know one another can come together and mingle daily. This also correlates with his concept of society as a school; the units of social cohesion in the future, as he sees it, will be thousands and thousands of small school districts throughout the country, in which every citizen during most of his life will be involved in the educational process. "And the beautiful thing," he says, "is that actually this would not be a school, it would be a playground! I'm antagonistic to schools. I am afraid of schoolteachers and intellectuals—I think they make the worst tyrants in the world, and they never have any understanding of the masses. But what I came to realize is that when you have a small school district of about four hundred people, what you really have is an *agora;* you have a small Athens, you have the ideal setup where people with different interests, different potentialities, different inclinations all meet each other, know one another, quarrel with each other, compete with each other, love each other, embrace and wrestle with each other. *This* is the creative situation."

Hoffer spends as much time as ever in libraries, doing research in his customary hit-or-miss fashion. "There's no system to it. I just cover the ground, go up all the blind alleys, and hope I'll be lucky." Occasionally he uses the university library at Berkeley, where he still goes one afternoon a week to meet and talk with students. With luck, he says, he may one day produce a book on the creative situation that will be comparable in scope to *The True Believer.* "But probably not," he adds somewhat ruefully. "In *The True Believer* I was at my best, my mind was at its best. *The True Believer* grew from within. I remember how I hated to finish it, how I would have loved to go on and spend the rest of my life writing that book."

All four of Hoffer's books have been selling at a phenomenal rate since the CBS program. Hoffer felt considerable anxiety for a while about the money he was making as a result— money he somehow seemed to consider unearned. His income has also been increased considerably by a syndicated column of Hoffer "Reflections" (culled mostly from his published writings and now appearing in more than seventy newspapers), and by his agreement with CBS for an annual, one-hour television dialogue with Sevareid. Asked why he had agreed to the annual TV exposure, Hoffer said that he thought he was entitled to blow off steam once a year. "I have all these things in me and there is a need to talk about them, to get them off my chest." He has overcome his worries about the money involved by using none of it on himself. He lives exclusively on his pension and his salary from Berkeley; everything else goes into a trust fund for young Eric Osborne and his family.

61

As the boy grows up, Hoffer sees correspondingly less of him. Like most families, the Osbornes have had their share of sadness. Their daughter, Toni, who never accepted Hoffer, left home after she finished school and went to New York. Her death in 1963, of a sudden and tragic illness, was almost more than Lili could bear. Steven, the older son, joined the Peace Corps after graduating from Berkeley and is now in Morocco. Selden and Lili Osborne have separated, although they remain friends. During the week Lili commutes every day to Redwood City, where she teaches a class of emotionally disturbed children in the public school. On weekends, though, the old, ramshackle Osborne house at the top of Clayton Street is a warm and pleasant place to be. Hoffer usually comes over for breakfast on Sunday. If the weather is good, he and Lili will take a long walk through the park—often the same, gradually descending path to the Pacific that he has traveled so many hundreds of times before. Hoffer loves the Golden Gate Park because it is entirely man-made; the fact that virtually every one of the thousands of shrubs, plants, and trees that grow there exists in a landscape created by man out of barren sand dunes fits in well with his theory that "man became what he is not with the aid of but in spite of nature."

It was only by cutting himself off from nature that man became what he is, Hoffer believes; man started to become human when he got out from under nature's inexorable laws, although in doing so he also made himself "an eternal stranger in this world." Nature—external and internal—remains the principal enemy of man. Hoffer developed a rather striking corollary to this theory one day not many years ago, when he visited the De Young Memorial Museum in Golden Gate Park with Lili and young Eric. Seeing the Indian and Chinese stone carvings of the Avery Brundage Collection, it suddenly occurred to him that when man wanted to depict the devil, he almost invariably made him in the image of bestial nature—with horns, tail, fur, and cloven hoof; God, on the other hand, had been created in the image of man himself. So far as Hoffer is concerned, nature is fine so long as it has been tamed and subdued by man. "No more picnics for me," he says, laughing.

After the Sunday-morning walk, Hoffer goes back to his room across town. He cannot be with people for too long at a stretch, not even the people he loves. He returns in the late afternoon and sits in the big, savory kitchen while Lili cooks one of her renowned dinners. People come in—teen-age friends of young Eric, students from the university, old friends of Lili's, sometimes one or more admirers of Hoffer's who have come long distances to see him. At these times Hoffer seems more like a benign paterfamilias than an adopted member of the family. He is relaxed and content. As he talks, his deep, German-accented voice rising and falling in sonorous rhythm, his eyes often closed tight upon the memory of what he is describing, one would not suspect his savage heart.

On a winter evening not long ago, after dinner at the Osbornes', Lili was telling a newcomer about the strange thing that happens when Hoffer lectures before an audience. It is not the same as when he speaks to friends, she explained, and it does not happen when he appears on television, although there are traces of it then. "It's rather frightening," she said. "The only thing I can compare it to is—well, lovemaking in public." Hoffer groaned and threw up his arms. "I was really quite upset about it at first," Lili continued, laughing, "because, you see, we'd never had to share him before. We'd always felt that Eric didn't belong to the world, he belonged to us. I remember the first time he was invited to speak in public, before the Unitarian Church here. He prepared himself beforehand—he even memorized what he was going to say and practiced it—and I thought he was going to sound just like a professor and bore everybody, so I didn't go. But the second time, at Stanford—tell him about that, Baba."

"That was something, yes," Hoffer agreed. "I was invited

by the Center for Advanced Study in the Behavioral Sciences down there. They wrote me a very good letter, so I went. And it turned out I was going to speak in that auditorium they have, set up on the hillside on top of everything. The walls are glass, and it was a clear day—you could see for miles. I didn't know what I was going to say. I hadn't prepared anything beforehand this time. But when I got up there, it was as though the whole state of California was spread out in front of me, and I suddenly had the idea of following my own train of thought that had led me to write *The True Believer*. I started way down in San Diego, and I told them how it began there, with my thinking about the undesirables and pioneers—and I didn't have to worry about what I was going to say next because I could just close my eyes and see how it was. I described the country in each place, where I got this idea, where I got that idea, how I followed the pea-picking all the way up from the Imperial Valley to just out-side Sacramento, how I went up into the mountains near Lake Tahoe looking for gold and discovered Montaigne, and then down to the San Joaquin and the cotton-picking, and the workmen's barracks outside Stockton where I wrote that sentence that actually appears in *The True Believer*—it was a regular safari. And, my God, sud-denly I had them eating out of my hand. I played with that audience. I'd call out, 'Anybody here from El Centro?' or 'Anyone from Indio? Anybody from Red Bluff?' and they responded; they were on the edge of their seats. It was something fantastic. Oh, I was in the mood for it. You have these moments of lucidity sometimes, moments when everything flows and your mind is just like a ballet dancer. The words come—it's happened to me several times. But I didn't like that feeling with the audience; it bothered me afterward, and I didn't speak again in public for a long time after that—not until a few years ago when I got all excited about automation. You see, the reason I don't think I'm an intellectual is that I'm not impressed by my ability to hold people with words."

64

Later, prompted again by Lili, Hoffer sang a song that came to him one day in the nineteen forties, when he was walking along a country road. A snatch of a tune that he had once heard a drunken Polish worker sing as he rolled naked in the snow suddenly popped into his head, and, without even thinking, he improvised the rest of the melody and found words to describe what he saw and felt, being "home on the road again." It was oddly moving—the sad, gypsy melody, the simple words sung in Hoffer's resonant bass, the emotional shadings he gave to it. "And you'd be surprised," he said afterward, "the flowers, the grass, the mountain peak, the foaming creek—they're all there. I could take you on that road tomorrow and you would see everything just as I had it. And I knew exactly what instruments there should be—the piano coming in here, the piccolo, the trumpet, and then, at the very end, the big bull fiddle. It was so natural. Even the one good sentence, about the 'joyous, winding, endless road that cares not where he goes and what his load'—it just came right out. You'd think if I could do that, I should go on doing it, but no. I never had the urge.

"And I don't believe there was anything unusual about my doing it. I'm not uncommon, you see. I'm a common man, and proud of my commonness. But talent is common, too—it's all around us, only most of the time it gets wasted. You just can't judge the intelligence, the talent of the American working masses by talking with them; you have to work with them to know that. I've worked with these people for forty-five years, and I've never ceased to learn from them. On the waterfront, you know, I never had a steady partner; always felt I ought to be able to work with anybody, and the technique I found for getting along with everybody was that you let them teach you. Everybody wants to teach, that's what I found out. Usually what they can teach is their languages. It's a regular League of Nations down there or it used to be when I first came. And it's strange, strange how things work out sometimes. I remember one

65

day, when I got down to the waterfront in the morning, everybody had paired off, and the only one that was left was a young Negro, very tall, very wild-looking, with scars all over his face. So I went to work with him. And the first thing that struck me was that he spoke with a beautiful Oxford accent. He was a Sudanese, a student who was working his way through college here, and they had given him a card so he could work on our waterfront. Being Sudanese, he was also a Moslem. And so I asked him to teach me that phrase you say when you become a Moslem—you know how it goes in English: 'I witness that there is no God but Allah,' and so forth. I wasn't thinking anything, I just asked him to teach me that phrase in Arabic, and it took me the whole day before I got it straight. '*Ashhadu an la'ilaha ill'Allah, wa ashhadu anna Muhammadan rasulu'llah.*' I remember I *labored* at it, but in the end I got it straight. It's a funny thing, too, they tell me that the only language I speak with any accent is English—I can speak snatches of Dutch, Spanish, French, Danish, Norwegian, even Japanese, all with no accent at all. Well, I forgot about that phrase. And then, one day, a few years ago, a foreign trade-union delegation came to San Francisco, and a couple of them said they wanted to meet me. So I went to meet them. And while I was there, a little Indonesian came walking up to me with a copy of *The True Believer* in his hand, and his finger pointing to a sentence there. Oh, you should have seen him! He had on that kind of glasses with a string that goes around the ear, and he came up on his high heels, cock of the walk, and said in a sort of whining voice, 'Mr. Hof-fair, you say here that our prophet Mohammed dangled loot before his followers. On what authority did you say that?' Well, I thought, you can't win no matter what you say to him; he's a regular two-bit intellectual. And then all of a sudden it came to me. '*Ashhadu an la'ilaha ill'Allah, wa ashhadu anna Muhammadan rasulu'llah!*' I hadn't thought of that phrase for years, but it came out letter perfect. Well, you ought to have seen his face. He practically fell into my arms. I told him, sure, you'd better be wary of us, you'd better be suspicious of us, because when your people find out the truth about America, they'll see that they can get along without intellectuals, just the way we've done over here. Oh, boy, I really wiped the floor with him. And he took it because of that phrase."

Hoffer beamed with pleasure at the recollection. "But it's true, what I told that little Indonesian," he said reflectively. "Some people try to tell me that the masses in Asia and other places are different from the masses here. Which I don't believe. I believe they're ninety per cent the same as here. And that's why all foreign intellectuals hate America—because we are the only real mass civilization that has ever existed, and our impulse is to do what's good for the masses and to say the hell with the intellectuals! It's the foreign intellectuals who are always the worst enemies of the masses. Look at that Sukarno, for example. When he first came on the scene, he told a newspaperman, 'I'm a double doctor—I've got two diplomas.' Look what Sukarno tells his people. 'How do we become a great nation?' he said. 'Do we need only rice and bread? A nation doesn't live only on rice and bread. A nation with a flaming spirit is a great nation. Our food is spirit.' Did you ever hear anything so stupid? Flaming spirit, my God.

"Of course, I know that now everything is changing here. The intellectuals are taking over, and the American masses are on the way out. There's been a new tilt to the social landscape in this country. Up until recently, most of the energy and ambition and talent in America found its main outlet in business. Lots of people who might have become intellectuals somewhere else went into mining, into engineering, into the struggle to pile up big fortunes. They set their hearts on toys, and that's always fine for the masses. The best condition for the masses is when the country is being run by people who set their hearts on toys. But now that's changing here. Since Sputnik, the social landscape in America has started to tilt

67

away from business, and the rewards offered to the intellectual have loomed higher and higher. I've read that according to a recent survey only twenty per cent of American undergraduates plan to go into business after college. The cold war between the intellectual and the bourgeois, which began in the nineteenth century, is coming to a climax in our time, and it's being won by the intellectual. Automation confirms it! But the solution is that society will become a school, and everyone will become an intellectual; and once everybody is an intellectual, we won't have to worry about the intellectuals any more!"

Hoffer sat in an arm chair by the big window in the living room, smoking a cigar and looking out over the rooftops of houses and the distant shimmer of lights on the bay. "Lili says I've led a sheltered life," he said quietly. "Can you beat that—after all those years on the bum? But in some ways I suppose she's right. I've never had the urge to see other places, other countries. In fact, I've only been outside of this country once in my life, for five minutes. It was in the thirties. I was working in the fields, down near the Mexican border, and one day out of curiosity I walked across the bridge at Mexicali. I took one look down an alley, saw the cobblestone streets, the crumbling buildings, smelled the stink, felt the weight of it crushing me down—and I turned around and ran back over the bridge. I felt as if I'd be put in jail or something and never get out. No, you just cannot conceive what this country has meant to the common man. Imagine writing a book about America and not mentioning kindness! So many people think they understand us, but I always say that Americans are the strangest, the most mysterious people on the face of the earth, and I still believe that. I don't believe we are falling apart. I think we are going to solve these problems confronting us, and that if we don't, then nobody will. This is all I know for sure."

APHORISMS

That which is unique and worthwhile
in us makes itself felt
only in flashes.
If we do not know how to catch
and savor these flashes,
we are without growth and
without exhilaration.

Man is the only young thing in the world.
all other forms of life.
man has in common with other living

A deadly seriousness emanates from
The cry of pain and of fear
things, but he alone can smile and laugh.

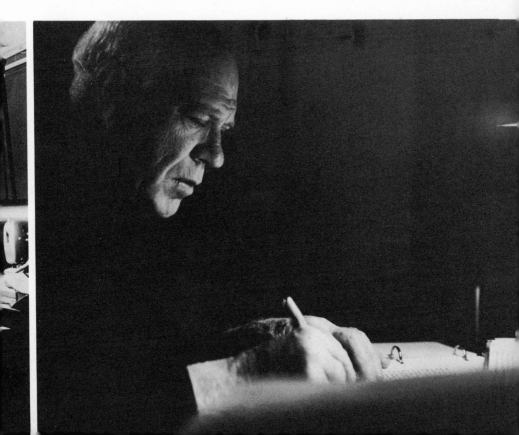

The intellectual will feel at home
where an exclusive elite
is in charge of affairs, and
it matters not whether it be an elite
of aristocrats, soldiers,
merchants, or intellectuals.
He would prefer an elite
that is culturally literate,
but will put up with one that is not.
What he cannot endure
is a society dominated by common people.
There is nothing
he loathes more than government of and
by the people.

When skills and experience
are made obsolete
by drastic change,
the dividing line between
grown-ups and the young
becomes blurred.
Yet this is the time when
the antagonism between generations
is likely to be greatest.
The young are in desperate straits
in an age of not knowing,
when the old no longer think
themselves in possession of the true
and only view possible
for sensible people, and growing up
becomes meaningless.

Sensuality reconciles us with the human race.
The misanthropy of the old is due in large part to
the fading of the magic glow of desire.

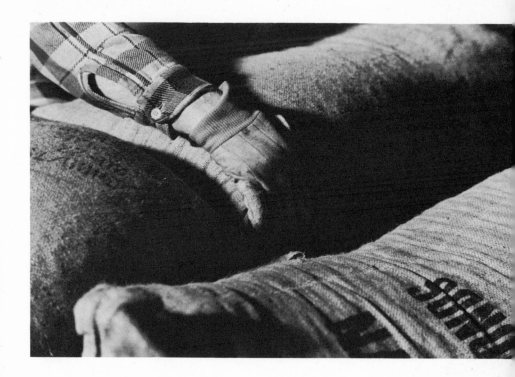

When we begin to think that most people
are no better than we,
the world seems full of people who
are fairly unpleasant.

History will come to an end either when the world
becomes a menagerie
or when man becomes fully human.
For history is the history of humanization;
of man's tortuous ascent through the millennia,
of his ceaseless effort
to break away from the rest of creation
and become an order apart.

People who lust for power
are not likely to be happy in America.
Here neither money nor education
equips a man for the attainment of power.
The opportunities in America
are for learning, experience, money,
achievement, comfort, freedom,
but not for power.

When trying to determine the role Christianity played
in the rise of the modern Occident,
it is necessary to remember that it was a weakening
of the Christian faith that marked the birth
of our present civilization.
The loss of religious faith was probably more
decisive than any peculiarly Christian
doctrine or attribute.
Most often when we renounce a faith,
we do not cast it off, but swallow it:
We substitute the self for the abandoned holy cause.
Hence the weakening of an ardent faith
may result not in lethargy but in an intensification
of the individual's drive.
What is decisive is not that we are without
a religious faith, but that we had
a god and lost faith in him.
It is this rejection and usurpation of a once
ardently worshiped god which has
had fateful effects on society and the individual
in the modern Occident.

To feel wholly at home
in this world is to partake
of the nature of plants
and animals.
Man is an eternal stranger
in this world.
He became a stranger
when he cut himself off from
the rest of creation
and became human.
From this incurable strangeness
stem our incurable
uncertainty, our unfulfillable
craving for roots,
our passion to cover the world
with man-made compounds,
our need for a God
who appoints us as His viceroy
in earth.

There is probably
an element of malice
in our readiness
to overestimate people—
we are, as it were,
laying up for ourselves
the pleasure of later cutting
them down to size.

Both the revolutionary
and the creative individual
are perpetual juveniles.
The revolutionary
does not grow up because
he cannot grow,
while the creative individual
cannot grow up because
he keeps growing.

Man learned to paint, carve, sculpt, and model in clay
long before he made a pot or wove cloth
or domesticated an animal. Man as an artist is infinitely
more ancient than man as a worker.
The prevailing opinion seems to be that man's ascent
through the millennia has been a grim affair.
We picture to ourselves the life of earliest man as
unimaginably hard and dangerous, a violent and
protracted duel, always facing the problem of how to eat
without being eaten, never knowing, on retiring, whether he
would be there in the morning. Yet as we trace back
the aptitudes, skills, and practices which enabled man to
survive and gain mastery over his environment,
we always reach
the realm of play. Most utilitarian devices
and inventions had their birth in nonutilitarian pursuits.
The first domesticated animal—the dog puppy—
was not the most useful but the most playful animal.
Man's inventiveness and his flashes of insight come not when
he is grubbing for necessities but when he reaches out
for the superfluous and the extravagant.
Play is older than work, art older than production for use.
Man was shaped less by what he had to do than by
what he did in playful moments.
Hence it is reasonable to assume that the humanization of man
occurred in surroundings where nature was bountiful and
man did not have to fight her tooth and nail.
The ascent of man was enacted in something like an Eden
playground rather than on a desolate battlefield.

It seems that the most important
revolutions are those other
people make for us.
The French Revolution altered
France relatively little,
but it created Germany.
Similarly, the
fateful consequences of
the Russian Revolution will be
a United Europe and
a new China.
The revolutionary nature of
the Negro Revolution
will manifest itself more in
its effects on the white
students and juveniles
than in a transformation of
the Negro's existence.

It is too late in the day for Americans to try
to win anyone with words, and it is even more certain
that we cannot win by giving.
What then can we do?
We can win the world only by example—
by making our way of life as good as we know how.
Our main problem is not the world but ourselves, and
we can win the world only
by overcoming ourselves.

The American is much better than his words.
In other civilizations it is legitimate to assume
that what people profess is on a higher level
than what they practice.
With the mass of people in America it is the
other way around: Their acts are more sensitive
and original than their professed opinions.
They practice, as it were, an inverted hypocrisy.

It is doubtful whether the oppressed
ever fight for freedom.
They fight for pride
and for power—

power to oppress others.
The oppressed want above all to
imitate their oppressor;
they want to retaliate.

The contemporary explosion of avant-garde innovation

in literature, art, and music

is wholly unprecedented.

The nearest thing that comes to mind is

the outburst of sectarian innovation at the time of

the Reformation, when every yokel felt competent

to start a new religion.

What is there at present in the cultural sphere which

corresponds to the shattering of an authoritarian

church in the sixteenth century?

Obviously, what our age has in common with the age of

the Reformation is the fallout of disintegrating values.

What needs explaining is the presence

of a receptive audience.

More significant than the fact that poets write

abstrusely, painters paint abstractly, and

composers compose unintelligible music is that people

should admire what they cannot understand;

indeed, admire that which has no meaning on principle.

The God who created nature was above all
a supreme technician.
But once He had created nature and automated it,
God lost interest in His creation.
It bored Him, and in His boredom God became an artist.
The God who created man was above all an artist,
and He created man in His own image—
the image of an artist.
All other animals are perfect technicians,
each with its built-in tool kit, each an accomplished specialist.
Man is a technically misbegotten creature,
half finished and ill equipped, but in his mind and soul
are all the ingredients of a creator, of an artist.
And it was God's mark as a supreme artist that
He refused to automate man.

The remarkable thing is that
it is the crowded life
that is most easily remembered.
A life full of turns, achievements,
disappointments, surprises, and
crises is a life full of landmarks.
The empty life has even
its few details blurred and cannot be
remembered with certainty.

One of the chief problems a modern society has to
face is how to provide an outlet for the
intellectual's restless energies yet deny him power.
How to make and keep him a paper tiger.

Suppose you come to San Francisco looking for
a person whose address you don't know....
My way is to stand on the corner of Powell and
Market and wait for him to come by.

And if you have all the time in the world
and you are interested in the passing scene,
this is as good a way as any ; and if you don't meet him,
you are going to meet someone else.

Man's thoughts and imaginings are the music drawn
from the taut strings of the soul.
The stretching of the soul that produces music is
the result of a pull of opposites—
opposite bents, attachments, yearnings.
Where there is no polarity—where energies
flow smoothly in one direction
—there can be hustle and noise but no music.

They who lack talent expect things
to happen without effort.
They ascribe failure to a lack of inspiration
or of ability, or to misfortune,
rather than to insufficient application.
At the core of every true talent
there is an awareness of the difficulties
inherent in any achievement, and the
confidence that by persistence and patience
something worthwhile will be realized.
Thus, talent is a species of vigor.

It is startling to realize that between 1400 and 1800 A.D.
the Eastern influence on the West was far greater
than the Western influence on the East.
Were it not for the Eastern influence, Columbus
might not have set out to discover America.
It is well to remember that Asia gave
us the instruments—gunpowder, the compass,
the astrolabe—with which to subdue it.

It is a sign of creeping inner death
when we no longer can praise the living.

In human affairs every solution
serves only to sharpen
the problem,
to show us more clearly what
we are up against.
There are no final solutions.

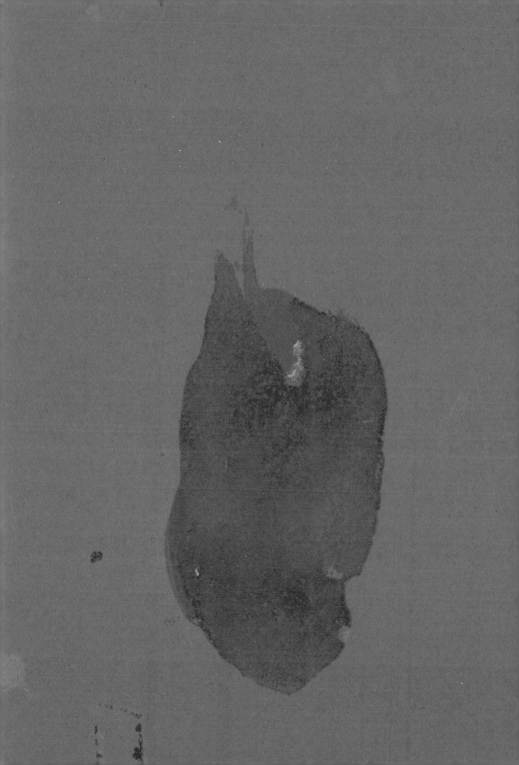